Yosemite's Historic Wawona

GILLFILLAN

Yosemite's Historic Wawona

The Wawona Tree

by Shirley Sargent

FLYING SPUR PRESS • YOSEMITE, CALIFORNIA

YOSEMITE'S HISTORIC WAWONA
by Shirley Sargent

Copyright 1979 by Flying Spur Press

Some photo credits in this book are abbreviated YNP for Yosemite National Park YPC&Co. for Yosemite Park & Curry Company, SS for Shirley Sargent, and WWH for Wawona Washburn Hartwig.

FIRST EDITION

FRONTISPIECE: In June, 1900, the first automobile to visit Yosemite, a two-cylinder Locomobile driven by Oliver Lippincott, was photographed driving through the famed Wawona Tunnel Tree (see page 54). The tree would be the site of many thousands of later photographs, as nearly every tourist who entered the Mariposa Grove wanted a pictorial record of the occasion. (Los Angeles County Museum of Natural History Collection.)

BOOK DESIGN by HANK JOHNSTON

Published by
FLYING SPUR PRESS
Box 278   Yosemite, Ca. 95389

Contents

•

Foreword

•

Wawona, cradled between the Mariposa Grove of Big Trees and the Yosemite Valley, is a tranquil spot: the long meadow, green lawns, and deer grazing peacefully on the golf course; the venerable hotel buildings, reminiscent of a bygone era; the Pioneer Village; the old covered bridge spanning time as well as the Merced River; forested hillsides, and the high mountains standing guard as they have for centuries.

Its history, however, is a robust one — a veritable microcosm of the country's westward expansion with all the adventure, ideals, and problems of that era. Vanquished Indians. Early settlers and homesteaders. Hardy men and women pioneers turned innkeepers and road builders, people of unbridled enthusiasm and vision who were propelled by an honest desire to share the beauty of the land they loved and the ever-increasing demands for better roads and more accomodations as Yosemite Valley became world famous. Exciting days of horse stages, with hold-ups and runaways. Cavalry troops. Famous guests and colorful characters. Expansion, followed by years of depression, war, and eventual renewal. Now the modern period of environmental awareness.

Did those early days open up a Pandora's box? Who knows, but Shirley Sargent, the Yosemite enthusiast and author of many books on the area. In *Yosemite's Historic Wawona* she has told a remarkably accurate history of Wawona, and told it with verve, heart, and understanding.

An English gentleman traveling the West in the early 1900's told my grandmother, "Your Wawona is like a bright green emerald set between the sparkling diamonds of Yosemite Valley's waterfalls and the red rubies of the Sequoias in the Mariposa Grove." A lovely compliment, in language so typical of the period.

I was born at Wawona, and lived there the first twenty years of my life, and, although my home has been elsewhere since then, a part of my heart has never left. All who read *Yosemite's Historic Wawona* will be grateful to Shirley Sargent, as I am, for the telling of this story. Let these pages be your stereoscope viewer to the past and present — and perhaps, the future — of one of California's "jewels."

Wawona Washburn Hartwig

OPPOSITE: The Big Trees of the famed Mariposa Grove drew attention to neighboring Wawona at an early date. (Ted Orland photograph.)

SECTION OF YOSEMITE NATIONAL PARK
BOUNDARY CHANGE 1932

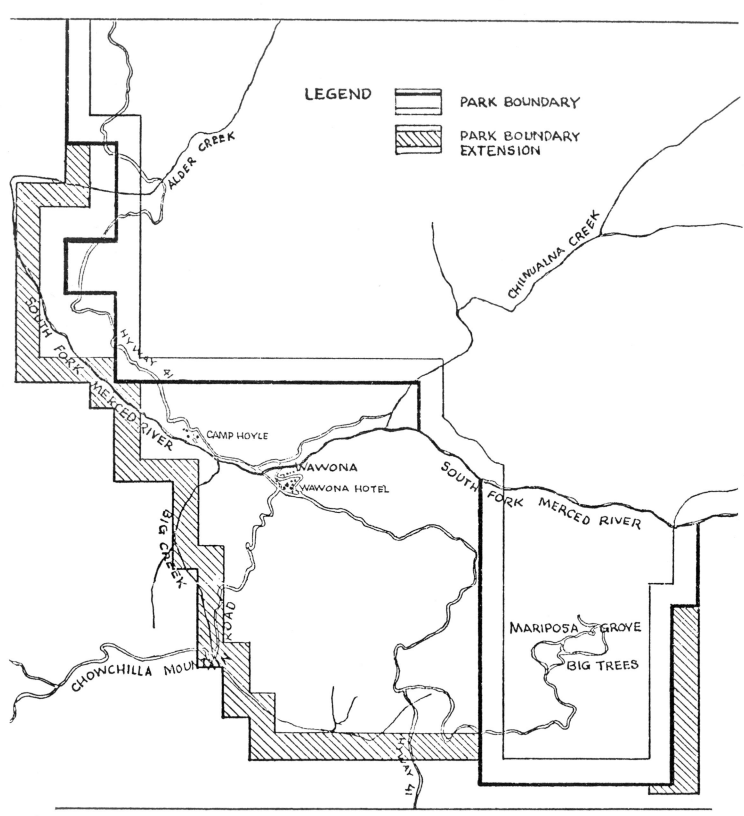

Preface

•

Since childhood, Wawona's white-painted, New England-type hotel buildings, the drowsy yet invigorating air, the massed pines, and the meadow, alternating between wild grasses and smooth golf greens, have fascinated me. My first substantial historical work was *Wawona's Yesterdays,* a booklet published in 1961 and still in print. As it contains only brief background on the hotel and the Washburns, the longtime owners, I felt compelled by profession and passion to prepare a more complete history. In 1973, I began episodic research; in 1974 I met endearing Wawona Washburn Hartwig who had been born and raised at Wawona; and in 1977, I started this book. Throughout the years, I have stayed at the hotel, explored its buildings, grounds, and the roads and trails of the Wawona Basin in company with Mrs. Hartwig, Al Gordon, Dean Shenk, and Marie Escola, and taught two university extension courses on Wawona's history. In addition, I rode an open-sided stage over the historic Chowchilla Mountain Road, visited Raymond, and followed other old roads.

Research took me to the Bancroft and California State Libraries, the Madera County Historical Museum, the Yosemite National Park Reference Library, the Yosemite Park and Curry Co. archives, the Mariposa County Historical Society, and the Mariposa Courthouse and nearby Hall of Records.

In the original drafts of this book, I included source notes to document the text, but the citations grew to so many pages, they had to be eliminated. Nevertheless, out of gratitude, I want to acknowledge some of the people and places that yielded facts, dates, anecdotes, and illustrative materials to me. From inception to publication, Mrs. Hartwig has been wholeheartedly supportive, sharing her own memories, her father's diaries, family pictures, and even typing my manuscript.

Eleanor Sell Crooks, a charming, knowledgeable oldtimer, who taught me the difference between open-sided stages, such as the Washburns used, and stagecoaches, was a great help, also. Al Gordon, Hester Stephan, Norman May, and Lou Stockton, present day Wawona residents, patiently answered my questions. Indefatigable historian Bertha Schroeder helped me with Mariposa background, and Mary and Bill Hood provided material on Yosemite's early days. Before their deaths, Clarence Washburn, Will Sell, Jr., Jay C. Bruce, and Hattie Bruce Harris contributed enormously of their knowledge of pioneer years. Horace Albright, Oliene Tresidder Mintzer, Hil Oehlmann, John Bingaman, Elsie Hoyle, Erma Murphy Fitzgerald, George Murphy, Wendell Otter, Dick Connett, Rosella Armstrong, Roberta Phillips, Sam Conway, Jean Bennett, Jr., Bob LaCroix, the present staff of the Wawona Hotel, Jack Hicks, Bill Germany, Rick Vocelka, Ed Hardy, and many others gave me information. Jack Gyer, Steve Medley, and Mary Vocelka of the Yosemite National Park Reference Library and Archives were particularly helpful in finding documentation. Gladys Hanson of the San Francisco Public Library, Virginia Ried and staff of the San Joaquin Valley Information Service, Debra Kroon of the Yosemite Park and Curry Co., and Chris Ortiz answered my pleas for data.

Objective eyes and red-penciling were derived from Barbara Billeter, the Hoods, B Weiss, Ann Matteson, and Hank Johnston. And finally, I owe appreciation to Wawona itself, for supplying the inspiration and the impetus for this book.

Shirley Sargent
February, 1979

Chilnualna Falls, less than two miles east of the Wawona Road, is one of the prime scenic attractions of the Wawona area. This photograph, taken in 1891, shows the six upper cascades. (Huntington Library Collection.)

CHAPTER I

Pallahchun

•

"Wawona Meadows themselves might be called the Sleepy Hollow of the West," claimed author J. Smeaton Chase in his 1911 book, *Yosemite Trails.* "It is the most peaceful spot that I know of in America and comes near being the most idyllic spot I have ever seen anywhere . . . Here is an unbroken meadow, green as heaven, a mile-long, waving knee-high with all delicious grasses and threaded with brooklets of crystal water. It is surrounded with a rail fence that rambles in and out and round about and hither and thither in that sauntering way that makes a rail-fence such a companionable thing . . . Beyond the fence the forest rises on all sides, surging gloriously up, ridge upon ridge, a most friendly and comfortable sight."

"A charm of birds," the "spirituous pungency" of pine resin, and "the voice of the river" also thrilled Englishman Chase. Nowhere in his narrative, however, did he mention the sounds and sight of cattle; or horses that grazed the grasses; or the grain fields, potato patches, and apple orchards that were an inherent part of the rural scene. Nor did he describe the complex of buildings and activity of the Wawona Hotel on the rising ground overlooking the meadow. James M. Hutchings, another Englishman, had portrayed it in his 1886 book, *In The Heart of The Sierras:*

"The very instant the bridge is crossed, on the way to the hotel, the whole place seems bristling with business, and business energy. Conveyances of all kinds, from a sulky to whole rows of passenger coaches

. . . come into sight . . . Hay and grain wagons; freight teams coming and going; horses with or without harness; stables for a hundred animals; blacksmiths' shops, carriage and paint shops, laundries and other buildings look at us from many different stand-points . . . that which now most claims our attention, and invites our sympathies, is the commodious and cheery, yet stately edifice in front of us known as the Wawona Hotel . . ."

Had not the Mariposa Grove of Big Trees (called "botanical prodigies" by Hutchings) existed only six miles away by stage road in one direction, and Yosemite Valley, the crown jewel of the Sierra, 25 miles to the north, Wawona might never have developed into a resort area of convenience and importance.

To Indians the verdant, 4,000-foot elevation meadows, the boisterous river, granite rocks, groves of oak and pine trees, and abundant game had been an idyllic campsite for eons. There the men hunted and fished while the women prepared acorn foods and wove intricate baskets for a variety of uses. Their name for the area was Pallahchun (a good place to stop) for it was a logical midway site between the foothills and Yosemite Valley, which they called Ah-wah-nee — deep, grassy valley.

On March 24, 1851, Major James D. Savage, his staff, and two companies of volunteers, 134 men in all, were the first white men to "stop" at Pallahchun. As the Mariposa Battalion, they had been commanded by

11

This romanticized view of the Wawona Hotel in 1886 was sketched by famed landscape artist Thomas Hill for James M. Hutchings to use in his book In the Heart of The Sierras.

the governor of California to subdue, capture, and take Indians, some of whom had attacked miners, to foothill reservations. At what is now public Camp A.E. Wood, on the South Fork of the Merced River a mile north of Wawona, a small band of Nuchu Indians surrendered. After that, the Battalion followed an Indian trail into Yosemite Valley, where they continued their pursuit and named outstanding features.

The Battalion's march to and from the region around Mariposa, a mining town, established a trail along the old Indian routes. Four years later, Indian guides led four separate parties, totaling 40 white men, principally miners, over the trail to Yosemite Valley. James Hutchings was a member of the first party in July, 1855, and, until his death in 1903, was associated with Yosemite Valley as hotelkeeper, guardian, tub-thumper, and author. Milton and Houston Mann, of the third party, were also later involved when they built the Mann Brothers Toll Trail from Mariposa to Yosemite Valley in 1856-57.

Galen Clark, a 42-year-old New Englander, was among the 17 miners from Mariposa who composed the second party of sightseers. Ever afterward, he, too,

was to be identified with Yosemite and Wawona, where he was a pioneer homesteader. In 1856 he suffered what he described as "a severe attack of hemorrhage of the lungs and was given up to die at any hour; and I went to the mountains to take my chances of dying or growing better which I thought were about even." The place he chose was the meadow and forest adjacent to the South Fork of the Merced where his party had camped in 1855. He filed a land claim for 160 acres there, in March, 1856, set up camp, and set out bareheaded "and some of the time barefooted" to regain health. Fifty-four years later, four days short of his 96th birthday, he died!

In April, 1857, he built his first 12′ x 16′ log cabin near a spring on the west end of the meadow. There he roughed it, fishing and hunting. As the Mann Brothers trail ran near his place, it was inevitable that the few travelers would stop there. "On their return trip," Clark recalled, "they would be out of provisions, and, as I always had a good supply of fresh venison and trout, they would call on me for meals."

That was the beginning of Clark's Station, predecessor of the Wawona Hotel, but not on the site so well known now. Date of Clark's move to the far side of the meadow is unknown, but it was probably before June, 1859. At that time Jessie Benton Fremont camped on the river bank, "dining sumptuously," she said, "on broiled squirrels and baked potatoes around Clark's campfire." This indicates that his "inn" was on the opposite side of the meadow closer to the river by that time.

Next day, he guided the Fremont party through the Sequoias, which he and Milton Mann had discovered in 1857. An admirer suggested Clark's Grove as a name, but he scorned that and named it the Mariposa Grove, although Indians told him their word for big tree was Wah-wo-nah.

Their name of Pallahchun for the area was soon forgotten as Clark's name was appended to meadow, ranch, inn, and the log bridge he built across the South Fork in 1858. By 1862, a traveler recorded that two tents, a log cabin, and bark lodges belonging to Indians were in the compound, called most commonly Clark's Station. Old photographs show that two more structures were added to make one long, low building connected with a shed-roof porch in front.

Most travelers came in the spring to avoid hot weather and dusty trails and to view the Valley's waterfalls in frothing, thundering glory. It is probable that an average of only 75 persons a year stayed at Clark's, but April-through-June travel taxed his resources. As early as 1863, a traveler was concerned that Clark's charge of four bits a meal was too small. Another 1864 visitor said there was "dust everywhere and buildings for the kitchen and accommodation of the ordinary backwoodsman were clustered about in the midst of an inclosure, in which and beyond as far as eye could see were stately trees but no grass anywhere."

Geologists, engineers, botanists, photographers, and politicians were influenced by Clark's thorough knowledge of the Yosemite region; he helped shape the opinion that both the Yosemite Valley and the Mariposa Grove required safeguarding. Jessie Fremont, Thomas Starr King, I.W. Raymond, Fredrick Law Olmsted, and other farseeing citizens inspired a Congressional Bill that created the Yosemite Grant. President Lincoln signed the bill granting the unique Valley and Grove to the State of California ". . . upon the express conditions that the premises shall be held for public use, resort, and recreation; shall be inalienable for all time . . ."

Since the State Legislature met only every two years, California's acceptance of the historic act could not take place until April, 1866. In the interim, the Governor appointed eight prominent Californians as Yosemite Valley Commissioners to minister the Grant. Galen Clark was among them. After the Legislature accepted the Grant, the Commissioners appointed Clark as Guardian. The five-hundred dollars a year allowed him had to be shared with a sub-guardian who was to reside in the Valley. Besides superintending,

Proximity of the Mariposa Grove of Sequoias, which Galen Clark discovered in 1857, helped make his inn a popular overnight stop. (Putnam and Valentine, 1901; SS Collection.)

Clark's duties included repairing and maintaining bridges and trails, stopping campers from cutting trees or making fires in grassy areas, and placating irate settlers. Hutchings, and others, fought eviction from the acreage they had pre-empted in Yosemite Valley.

So time-consuming was the new position that Clark could not adequately fulfill both the Guardian's job and that of innkeeper. Although he spent much of his time and labor at Clark's Station, he leased it out in 1868 and 1869. What money he earned financed improvements to his business, additions to his land holdings, and creation of access roads.

Stage roads were the key to tourist trade. Thanks to widespread publicity and photographs of the Yosemite Grant's unique scenic masterpieces, knowledge of it, (and the desire to see it), was world-wide. There were three pioneer trails into Yosemite Valley, two from the north benefiting Stockton, Modesto, and Coulterville, and the Mann Brothers trail from Mariposa on the

After 1874, Yosemite Guardian Galen Clark lived in Yosemite Valley where his crony George Fiske, the Ansel Adams of the era, took this springtime view. (SS Collection.)

south. Naturally, ranchers, innkeepers, and merchants along each route banded together to build toll roads to alleviate tourist inconveniences, and at the same time attract their trade. Their efforts intensified as the transcontinental railroad approached Sacramento, and the Central Pacific planned a line down the San Joaquin Valley. Completion of that project would make Yosemite even more accessible, and whichever stage route was completed first would be pre-eminent.

Mariposans had assumed that the State Legislature would appropriate funds to build a wagon road to the Mariposa Grove since it was an important part of the Yosemite Grant, but bills failed to pass. Galen Clark, himself, spent money and energy each spring on repairs and improvements on the trail, aided, at times, by subscriptions from Mariposa businesmen. By 1866, a stage road terminated about twelve miles west of Clark's Station, but neither private, state nor county funds were made available to close the gap.

Finally, in March, 1869, Clark organized a turnpike company and a survey was made. "Success to the enterprise, we say!" said the *Mariposa Gazette,* but the company needed more tangible backing. "Either money, work, or anything else that will give material aid will be most thankfully received and economically expended," Clark pleaded in a letter to the public published in the December 17, 1869, *Gazette.* "Are the people living on the Mariposa route to Yo Semite Valley willing to lose the travel rather than assist in making a wagon road further to the place! . . ."

His appeal and influence resulted in the organization of a new company in February, 1870. Backers included prominent businessmen in Mariposa and Stockton who owned the stage line between the two towns. John Wilcox, a Mariposa businessman and politician, was elected president, Edwin Moore, Mariposa County Recorder, secretary, and Galen Clark, treasurer. They hired a powerfully built ex-miner named John Conway, who possessed strength, verve, and engineering skill, to direct the construction, which began almost immediately.

Stockton associates were strong allies, for Stockton, an established port city, was reached by railroad as well. Many Yosemite-bound people arrived there by boat or train, stayed at the elegant new Yo Semite House Hotel, and left in stages operated by N. Z. Fisher. As anticipated, the 1869 completion of the overland railway greatly increased travel to Yosemite (from 623 visitors in 1868 to 1122 in 1869). It followed that tourists, largely wealthy Easterners or foreigners, would expect service and comfortable stages.

Clark's Station had opened in May, 1870, under the management of Huldah and Edwin "Deacon" Moore. On December 9, 1869, Clark had sold Moore half-interest in his buildings, land, and the South Fork toll bridge for $2,000. That was one-third of his share of the road construction cost; he had to mortgage his half of the property, called Clark and Moore's, to finance

14

Heart of Wawona's charm is its verdant meadow. (Ansel Adams photograph, circa 1933, YPC & C Co. Collection.)

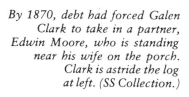

By 1870, debt had forced Galen Clark to take in a partner, Edwin Moore, who is standing near his wife on the porch. Clark is astride the log at left. (SS Collection.)

15

The South Fork of the Merced bisects the Wawona with might and beauty. A white cascade of Chilnualna Falls appears on the mountainside. (Putnam and Valentine, 1901; SS Collection.)

the balance. Despite the new debt, Clark was enthusiastic as he noted the tolls collected on road and bridge (even a man on foot had to pay $1.00), the lodging and meal charges paid by people who overcrowded their facilities, and the popularity of the Moores. The place had needed a woman's touch, he felt, and the couple's presence meant that he could be away, working as Guardian, without concern. He and Moore had a water-powered sawmill built that season, which meant substantial, better-looking improvements could be made.

Even though two of Clark's children had arrived to help, and visitation increased each year, and despite the fact that famed guests such as Ralph Waldo Emerson, Grace Greenwood, Joaquin Miller, and Asa Gray boosted his place in talk and text, Clark's debts grew higher. The State Legislature did not buy his toll road as he had hoped, nor did the state regularly pay his salary as Guardian. Clark added to his own financial problems by contracting to buy more land and making abortive mining investments. Between 1867 and 1872, Clark mortgaged his land and improvements four times for sums totalling $10,700. No record exists of the money he borrowed from relatives and friends, but it

was apparently a considerable amount.

In 1874 both the Coulterville and Big Oak Flat roads entered Yosemite Valley in June and July respectively; this inevitably meant that most tourists elected to travel those routes rather than endure twenty-four miles in the saddle on the South Fork Trail. In 1873 Clark and Moore had paid John Conway for a road survey over the southside route and then tried to interest the State Legislature in financing it. "The Act to provide for the construciton of a wagon road into Yosemite Valley," *Gazette* editor L. A. Holmes reported, "died a miserable death . . ."

Undeniably, Clark and Moore's trade was hurt, which meant their debts increased. It was not a profitable summer. Winter was worse, for the house of mortgages collapsed. On December 26, 1874, Clark and Moore's was sold for a paltry $1,000 and cancellation of the $20,000 owed the firm of Washburn, Coffman & Chapman.

Clark moved to Yosemite Valley as full-time Guardian, and husband to an improbable second wife. Behind him he left a collection of buildings, a sawmill, a blacksmith shop, a lengthy water ditch, seventeen years of failure, and an abundance of good will.

CHAPTER II

The Man from Putney

•

Galen Clark's successor at the South Fork was Albert Henry Washburn, who, even at 39, had a benevolent, patriarchal look, and a striking resemblance to General U.S. Grant. Washburn's civilian command, however, was in building roads and stage lines in Mariposa and Merced Counties. Like Clark, Washburn was a New Englander, but unlike Clark, he symbolized the shrewd, successful Yankee image.

At least six generations of Washburns had preceded him. Knight's Washbourne and Great Washbourne, neighboring villages near Worcester, England, commemorate the Washburn family whose members date back to the Twelfth Century. In 1635, a John Washbourne immigrated to New England, served as Secretary of the Massachusetts Colony, and founded the line of American Washburns that included congressmen, statesmen, governors, generals, and a contemporary historian.

A fifth generation descendant of John, named Seth Washburn, was born in Putney, Vermont, in 1788. Between 1811 and 1840, a year before he died, Seth sired fifteen children by two wives, a not unusual feat, but the fact that they were all sons might have merited him a place in the Guiness *Book of Records*. His first wife bore him eight sons, and his second had seven more.

All but the first two of the fifteen boys were born in the shadow of Vermont's famed Green Mountains in a farmhouse near Randolph, population about 2,000.

Seth Washburn was noted for his husbandry with soil and sons, all of whom learned as youngsters to plow, build rock fences, and milk cows.

The last five boys, Seth Caswell, born October 13, 1832, Edward Payson, born March 13, 1835, Albert Henry, born November 17, 1836, John Stephen, born December 30, 1838, and Julius Francis, born March 2, 1840, were close in age, looks, and interests. Their venturesome spirits were to affect the development of Mariposa County, California, a county and state not even founded until eight years after the birth of the youngest.

When Seth senior died in 1841, the older boys were on their own as farmers, Mrs. Washburn took the five youngest back to the Washburn farm in Putney in the fertile Connecticut River Valley near the border of New Hampshire. There the boys did farm chores on the large acreage, and attended the Washburn School, a brick building near the two-story Colonial home.

Seth Junior traveled to California before he was 20, presumably to better his uncertain health. He was listed as a clerk in Mariposa County in the 1852 census. By 1856, brother Edward had joined him at the mining settlement of Bridgeport, five miles from Mariposa, the county seat. Seth wrote his mother that the climate was "salubrius" compared to New England. In June, 1856, Edward told her they were doing a "good business" running a store, and, because a Sunday law was in effect, "relieved of the disagreeable necessity of

Bridgeport was on the decline when Carleton E. Watkins photographed part of it in 1860. (SS Collection.)

trading on Sunday." Despite unpaid accounts, the firm of Seth C. Washburn & Bros. prospered enough so that Henry, and possibly John came out, and ailing Seth traveled home to Putney, where he died nine months later. Ed and Henry were enumerated as merchants in the 1860 census.

Bridgeport was in live oak country along Agua Fria Creek. It boasted a couple of stores, the Washburn Mine and stamp mill, a scattering of rude frame buildings, and a population of placer miners. "Trade with the Chinamen is on the increase," Edward commented in May of 1859. "We are selling nearly twice the amount of rice than usual." When mining declined, so did Bridgeport. Only Henry Washburn remained, running the store, mining, and raising hogs. In late October, 1865, he borrowed $3,000 on his quartz veins, probably to finance a home, for he was engaged, the *Mariposa Gazette* said, to a lady "whose elegant poetical productions place her among first . . . writers in the State." Their marriage, of "no little moment" in Mariposa, took place December 18, 1865, when he was 29, and Jean Lindsay Bruce 27.

Her father, John J. Bruce, was Scottish, and her mother French, but she was a native of New York where she was born in 1838. Bruce and a brother had operated a steamship line between New York and England, and, later, invented a machine to make hard-tack. In 1852 gold had lured him to Mariposa. He was the father of nine, so Washburn acquired eight brothers-and-sisters-in-law when he married Jean. For the rest of his life, Washburn was associated with some of them as partner or employer. At the time of his

marriage, two of Jean's brothers, Charles and Albert, were running a machine shop in Mariposa, and sister Fannie, another poet, was living there with her husband, John Jay Cook. Cook was an affluent entrepreneur from New York who came to Mariposa in 1862, ran a drugstore, and was the Wells Fargo agent. Before long he spread financial wings in Merced and San Francisco. Later he would be intimately associated with Washburn in his rise to power.

Surprisingly, the terrible fire of August 1866, which destroyed 60 buildings in seven blocks in the central part of Mariposa, altered Washburn's residence, and advanced his career. Bruce Bros., Machinists, valued at $500, was burned out, as were John R. McCready's stables and Col. E.S. Terry's livery business. "Notwithstanding all of the livery Stables in town were destroyed during the fire, Fisher's stage line continued its regular course . . ." commented the *Mariposa Gazette*. Terry rented "a large and commodious building" at the corner of Bullion and Seventh Street, but wanted to quit. On January 30, 1867, he sold his business to Washburn for $2,400. Brother-in-law J.J. Cook had a financial and advisory interest, but Henry was the proprietor. Both men knew that Mariposa's importance as a midway stop and outfitting place for Yosemite-bound tourists was increasing yearly.

Nine days before Henry Washburn began his new profession, he and Jean were saddened by the death of an infant son. Although he lived less than a day, they named him Henry Campbell Washburn and later had a headstone erected over his grave in the Mariposa Cemetery. Jean's grief was poured out in a lengthy poem, but was assuaged by the birth of a daughter, Jeannie Bruce Washburn, in April, 1868. Her birth was celebrated by another poem titled "Our Darling."

Washburn rented horses, Concord wagons, carriages, buggies, and buckboards and outfitted saddle parties with mounts and "experienced guides." "Particular attention" boasted the weekly *Gazette* ad of Washburn and Cook, "paid to transient travel, and every attention paid to animals entrusted to our keeping." So successful was he in attracting customers that it became obvious to his rival, Jack McCready, that Mariposa was not big enough for two livery businesses. Accordingly, on April 9, 1868 Washburn and McCready joined forces, and the partnership with J.J. Cook dissolved, although the latter remained a friend and advisor. Born in Ireland, McCready had been raised in Pennsylvania, and, along with a plethora of relatives, was a Mariposa pioneer.

The new partners wanted a bigger piece of the tourist action and explored the possibility of operating a stage line. Until 1871, however, Fisher & Company stages from Stockton continued to carry all tourists to Mariposa and the South Fork, but beginning in May of that year, passengers could board one of Washburn & McCready's "first-class, easy-riding stages" for the last 26 miles to Clark & Moore's. Comfort was assured,

Clark's Station looked about like this when Henry Washburn took it over in January, 1875. (J.P. Soule publication, 1870; SS Collection.)

the *Gazette* noted, because Washburn & McCready had "received on Saturday last a splendid eleven-passenger stage which they immediately placed on the road. It runs smooth and is just the thing for the mountains."

McCready saw to rentals, care of the stock, and day-by-day livery business while Washburn was out on the road soliciting business, inserting ads in San Francisco newspapers, influencing people, buying horses and mules, ordering vehicles and generally acting as salesman, purchasing agent and publicity man.

As mentioned earlier, the completion of the transcontinental railway in May, 1869, had signaled an immediate increase in Yosemite visitation. Chinese workers subsequently laid rails south through the San Joaquin Valley and by December, 1871, had a new, though temporary, terminus that quickly became the hub of Merced City. Lots were surveyed and staked out

by the Central Pacific Railroad Company, which evolved into the Southern Pacific. On December 10, 1871, Washburn and McCready paid $750 for two and one-half lots just two blocks from the railroad station and the enormous El Capitan Hotel, which was being hurriedly built by the Central Pacific. (To fill the need for overnight lodging while the four-story building was under construction, the CPRR used a private palace car for rooms.) "Washburn and McReady (sic) are erecting sheds to serve as a livery stable," recorded the January 27, 1872, *San Joaquin Valley Argus*. The partners planned to operate a pioneer stage line between Merced, Mariposa, and the South Fork. Their only rival was Mark McClenathan of Modesto, who was also building a stable with the plan of running stages to Yosemite Valley via Coulterville.

Washburn hired men to run the new stable, but he wanted a loyal, trustworthy fellow like brother Ed as a

19

Mariposa's prosperity, pictured by Charles Bierstadt in 1860, was greatly diminished by a disastrous fire in August of 1866. Henry Washburn is third man from left. (Mary and Bill Hood Collection.)

In Putney Vermont, the Washburn home and barns were the huh of the 120 acre farm where thoroughbred Jersey cows, timber, and tobacco were raised. Part of the land is still owned by a descendant, and the remodeled house exists. (Courtesy of William Darrow.)

station agent. While Henry had prospered in Mariposa, he had kept in touch with his Vermont family. By August, 1870, only Julius was living on the family farm with his mother, his wife, and first child. He was a farmer as were John and Edward. Census records of 1870 show that John had land valued at $10,000 and a personal estate worth $2,100. He had married Nellie M. Taft in 1868, and their son, Arthur, was born three years later. At 35, Edward was still single and owned land valued at $12,000. Henry wrote Ed urging him to return west and work for Washburn and McCready.

Between them, Washburn and McCready had hired a group of outstanding stage drivers — talented, skillful men such as Hiram (Hi) Rapelje, George Monroe, and Billy Dowst. Likewise, guides who led tourists on the last, long horseback stretch to Yosemite Valley, had to be reliable, familiar with the trails, and reasonably entertaining. Pioneer guides were Joe Ridgeway, Eli Stump, known as (what else?) "a trump," Tom Tremea, and lively Pete Gordon. Pete's son, Tom, went to work for "Uncle Henry" while still a schoolboy. In all, four generations of Gordons were to work for, and be unstintingly loyal to, Washburn.

He earned loyalty from all his men by his fairness and his awareness of their services, for he saw them in action every time he was out on the road or trail, and that was often. Alone, with his wife or business associates, he made many trips into Yosemite Valley. From Clark and Moore's the trail aimed north, then east to Peregoy's Mountain View House, an overnight stopping place at 7,000' elevation. Mary, a renowned cook and baker, and Charles Peregoy ran their sixteen-bed inn from the fall of 1869 until 1878. During those years, they maintained a still extant guest register. Washburn was a frequent guest and signer. From Peregoy's the trail wandered through forests and winsome meadows, reaching the rim of the Valley 150 feet above what is now called Old Inspiration Point. From there it descended sharply to the Valley floor, just east of Bridalveil Fall.

There were three pioneer hotels bearing the names of their owners, Leidig's, Black's and Hutchings' in Yosemite Valley in the early 1870's. La Casa Nevada, a picturesque inn on the flat near the base of Nevada Fall, a place of delectable food and spirits, maintained a large register that is still preserved in the Yosemite

Archives. Drawings, verses, famous names, and some nonsense filled the pages. A. H. Washburn simply signed his name, adding date and residence. His wife, Jean was not so reticent. After their July, 1871, excursion into Little Yosemite Valley, she recorded her place names: "Diamond Shower Falls" in the eastern end . . . "a magnificent volume of water . . .", and "Jean's Dome." None of her titles gained recognition, but a niece claimed "Aunt Jeanne" had named Ribbon Fall in Yosemite Valley "Virgin's Tears" because "it dried up so fast." That title is still used by tour guides.

Washburn was so impressed with Little Yosemite Valley that he filed a possessory land claim in its upper end, and had a log cabin built there. It is probable that he envisioned a commercial venture in Little Yosemite, for trail builder John Conway recorded that he arrived at Liberty Cap, looming above Little Yosemite, in July, 1871, "to build stairway leading up to fit Yosemite proprietors A.H. Washburn and J.R. McRady. Completed October."

Washburn was at Clark and Moore's frequently, knew the pioneers well, and was familiar with their sorry business record, their debts, and lack of success in obtaining financial backing to finish a road between the South Fork and Yosemite Valley. He knew prospects for future business, once a stage road was open to the Valley, were excellent and anticipated the place could regain its share of the tourist trade. An overhaul was needed, particularly in the bookkeeping and accounting system; that, coupled with energetic management and some new buildings, could make the inn a first-class paying resort.

During 1874, Washburn contemplated taking over the mortgaged enterprise. Clark and Moore owed him an unknown sum, Hugh Davany, major Mariposa mortgage broker, a recorded $5,600, and other debtors. McCready's involvement in planning ended with his death August 12, 1874, two weeks after he suffered lung hemorrhage on his way to Clark and Moore's. Washburn needed a reliable man in Mariposa, and needed capital, so he considered possibilities carefully. Instead of one man, he selected two after he took them on inspection trips of Yosemite's roads, trails, and hotels.

Both of his new partners were hard-headed, practical men who possessed capital and enterprise. William F. Coffman, 40, had been a miner for 11 years before election as the County Assessor. Emery W. "Wash" Chapman was a pioneer businessman in Madera. They bought out McCready's half-interest, valued at $6,750, and Washburn retained his half. The new firm's primary objective was to complete the long-anticipated South Fork-Yosemite Valley Road and compete with the Coulterville and Big Oak Flat routes.

On November 2, 1874, they filed an application with the Mariposa County Supervisors to build the toll road. On December 12, Conway and Moore contracted with Washburn, Coffman, and Chapman to construct 16 miles of the proposed route for $10,000. Before the contract was announced, 40 Chinamen had pushed the road as far as Alder Creek, four miles from the South Fork. Finally, on December 26, the new partnership acquired Clark and Moore's for $21,000, according to the *Mariposa Gazette,* but the property deed recorded January 7, 1875, showed that only $1,000 cash changed hands. Up to that time, no one had made money on the South Fork enterprise, but Washburn was on the move.

CHAPTER III

The Road Builders

•

"The new road from the South Fork to Yosemite Valley is being pushed with determined zeal," proclaimed the January 9, 1875, *Mariposa Gazette,* "by men of indomitable energy possessed of ample means." Upwards of 100 men were at work on the road in unseasonably dry weather . . . "Death to farmers should it continue a month or two longer." The men of "indomitable energy" regarded the fair skies happily, and hired more Chinese to join their indefatigable brethren clearing roadbed. Their tools were rudimentary; axes, shovels, picks, and wheelbarrows. Black powder, which wasn't much stronger than gunpowder, was used to blast out immovable boulders. Literally thousands of rocks and trees had to be removed, several bridges and hundreds of feet of retaining walls built. Belated storms stopped work for a while, and ice and snow had to be removed before construction resumed.

John Conway, already Yosemite's master trail builder,* who had surveyed the road, was engineer and overall boss. Under him were James and Joe (short for Josephus) Ridgway, from Mariposa, who super-

---

*Conway engineered and directed the building of the still-used trail from Snow's Hotel near the base of Nevada Falls up over its top and into Little Yosemite Valley in 1871, the Four Mile Trail from the floor of Yosemite Valley to Glacier Point in 1871-72, and began another to the top of Yosemite Falls in 1873.

vised the work, done by two large crews of Chinese. One camp, directed by James, was near the Yosemite Valley end of the road; the other near Alder Creek at the South Fork end. Work thus proceeded simultaneously from both ends of the 23-mile road.

From Alder Creek, the road ran southerly on the western flank of the mountain, always up and down, from 4,000 to over 7,000 feet elevation, and finally turned easterly for the precipitous descent into Yosemite Valley. Grades averaged 8 per cent, but some, such as the last plunge, were up to 12 per cent. Width of the roadbed averaged 16 feet so teams going in opposite directions could squeak past at most places. Stages were seven feet wide, hub to hub, and freight wagons about the same.

No deaths were recorded among the workers, whose number increased to 300, but a Chinese woman camp follower was murdered, and a cash box containing a payroll of over $1,200 stolen. After that, a deputy sheriff organized a posse of stage drivers to guard the South Fork bridge, and they searched over 60 Chinamen before one balked at the "Throw down your bundle" command. A display of six shooters persuaded him to conform, and searchers found $815 in gold in his bundle.

Covered bridges were integral to Washburn's boyhood home, and when the hand-hewn timbers Clark had used to cross the South Fork needed repair, Washburn added sides and a roof to the 130-foot span. All

Top stagedrivers, like Uriah Tobey, shown here handled the reins on the final descent into Yosemite Valley. (George Fiske photograph; WWH Collection.)

Constructed between December of 1874 and June, 1875, the Wawona Road was used until 1933. (Dean Shenk picture, 1978.)

housing boards were cut in the sawmill Clark and Moore had built. Even then, the covered bridge was a rarity; today it is unique as the only covered bridge in a national park, and one of the few existing in California. For years, tolls were levied for its use.

While work proceeded, Coffman ran the firm's stables in Mariposa and continued his job as County Assessor, Chapman seems to have acted as a liaison man, and Washburn supervised the Merced enterprise when not on the road soliciting business. Brother-in-law J.J. Cook, who by then ran a drugstore in San Francisco, provided Washburn with headquarters in the City, and introduced him to men such as Charles Crocker, one of the "Big Four" of railroad building fame, and other equally influential figures. One source claimed that Crocker loaned Washburn money to help finance the new road.

Innkeeping on the South Fork was not a high priority with the new firm, but, under its new name, Big Tree Station, it remained open all winter for guests, to store supplies, and to distribute the payroll, which was in gold and silver coin.

"Milk will never sour in his cellar," said the *Gazette* in approving the retention of Edwin Moore as manager. His wife, the admirable hot-stove artist, Huldah, was a mainstay, too. They kept a list of winter arrivals, later published in the *Gazette,* which showed that a total of seven stayed there in February, 34 in March and 60 in April, the usual beginning of the tourist season. Stages carried passengers to the very heels of workmen; from these constantly-changing points horses were ridden.

Attendant to the progress of the road was the establishment of stations where horses could be changed. Because of steep grades, stage stops were placed about four miles apart, where water and a level spot was available. Distances were measured from Big Tree Station, elevation 4,000 feet. The first station was at Alder Creek, 4,800 feet, second Eight-Mile Station, 5,500 feet; third at Eleven-Mile Station, 5,750 feet; and fourth at Chinquapin Flat, 6,200 feet, 13 miles distant. From there the road continued its ups and downs to Fort Monroe, 5,540 feet, then descended to New Inspiration Point where the stage stopped for the first view of Yosemite Valley.

Each station had water, stables with a corral, a cabin, and a keeper. He anticipated the arrival of every stage, and had relay horses harnessed so they could be "swung in" with a minimum of delay. At some stops there was time for passengers to stretch their legs and find a tree, if not a privy. Many people traveling in private carriages, or afoot, camped near the stations. Fishing was good in both Alder and Eleven-Mile Creeks.

Washburn, Chapman and Coffman were eager to begin collecting tolls, so they appealed to the Mariposa County Supervisor who set the following charges on May 5, 1875.

For 62 years, the covered bridge, reminiscent of Henry Washburn's native Vermont, carried all traffic on the toll road. Today it is a link to the past, used by pedestrians and stages but not autos. (YNP Collection.)

Passenger team, per passenger	$1.00
Freight team, per animal	1.00
Horse and rider	1.00
Animals packed, per head	.75
Animals loose, per head	.75
Cattle, per head	.25
Foot passengers, each	.25

By April 18, the road was nearly completed and $35,000 had been spent by the gentlemen of (formerly) "ample means!" After the road rounded the last mountain shoulder high on the southern side of Yosemite Valley, it had to make a descent of 1,600 feet in 2.9 miles. Part of that distance was over precipitous slopes of loose, jumbled boulders. Creating a solid roadbed in heaped, unsteady rocks was an exacting and time-consuming job, stalling completion for weeks. Someone gave it the name of "Washburn Slide."

Disappointed but undeterred, Washburn, Chapman and Coffman ordered stages driven as far as New Inspiration Point, where passengers disembarked to "oh" and "ah" at the amazing view of the promised land, and then walked past the 300 yards still under construction. At the same time, workmen dismantled the stages, carried the pieces by hand past the unfinished section, and reassembled wheels, body, and seats. When the novel portage was finished, passengers cheered and climbed back in, horses were harnessed, and the last part of the ride enjoyed. The procedure followed for two months, was accomplished with remarkable speed and dexterity that never failed to excite onlookers. "Apparently the unusual nature of

this outweighed its inconveniences," Yosemite naturalist C. Frank Brockman wrote in 1943, "for it was claimed that many visitors selected this route because of the novelty."

In 1874, two tremendous celebrations, marking the opening of both the Coulterville and Big Oak Flat Roads, left dust clouds that lingered for days. Not to be outdone, an even grander celebration was planned to salute the opening of the southside road. Fifty Mariposans joined residents of the Yosemite Valley on five committees of preparation, and Stephen M. Cunningham, a pioneer of the Valley, was chosen to be Grand Marshall. Galen Clark, who served on the reception committee, and Henry Washburn probably refused the honor, for neither man enjoyed the limelight. The only committee on which Washburn, Chapman, and Coffman served was the one in charge of music. "This is a joke," commented the usually supportive *Gazette* editor, Angevine Reynolds. "We will wager a dozen bottles of Weiler's lager against a dozen Mariposa trout that neither of them can tell a tune played by a brass band or a fiddle from a bray . . ." Music, dancing, and speeches were to be included in the gala event.

After three changes, the date was set for Thursday, July 22, 1875. An impromptu celebration took place almost a month earlier, however, for June 24, 1875 was the day on which a stage actually crossed the arduously built roadway over Washburn Slide. A crowd had massed near the base of Bridalveil Fall, and when the stage braked to a dramatic stop, their shouts and yells nearly matched the thunder of the waterfall.

As fresh teams were needed about every four miles on the steep, new road, five stage stations were set up. This barn stood at Chinquapin. (WWH Collection.)

William Coffman climbed aboard and took the reins for the triumphal four and one-half mile journey on to Coulter and Murphy's Hotel, (formerly Hutchings Hotel,) where further celebration occurred and a telegram "announcing the glorious intelligences" was sent to the *Gazette*.

Of course the *Gazette* covered the July 22 festivities, even printing the names of 42 Mariposans who traveled to Yosemite Valley, equipped with "cordials and restoratives" on Washburn and Company stages. They admired the road's "fine engineering, and splendid construction with easy grade and passing through a continuous shade amidst the wildest and most beautiful scenery." Valley residents awaited the procession at Bridalveil where W.F. Howard of Yosemite gave the welcoming address, and Mariposa's State Assemblyman, J.W. Wilcox, who had backed the route since 1869, responded. Then the procession of about 250 people in vehicles and on horses, led by Grand Marshall Stephen Cunningham, formed. Men firing guns preceded it, the Yosemite Band marched in it, and the Merced Brass Band followed.

Leidig's and Black's Hotels, halfway up the Valley, "were appropriately decorated," as was Coulter and Murphy's which was headquarters for the remainder of the day. An archway, emblazoned with the names of pioneers, flags, and Chinese lanterns, welcomed the dusty procession.

About seven o'clock, after a salute from the artillery and music from the Merced Band, there were speeches by several prominent Mariposans and a poem read by Ida Howard, "all interspersed with tunes from the band." After that the crowd "crushed into and around" the Cosmopolitan Saloon and Bathhouse, which had been "transformed into a fairy palace" for dancing that continued all night.

Three cheers for Washburn, Chapman, and Coffman, and a sigh for Galen Clark, the pioneer who promoted the South Fork and Yosemite Turnpike Road, but could not finance it. The trio who did finance it must share credit with John Conway, James and Joe Ridgway, and the 300 Chinese workers as road builders. Although they were forgotten, their road was an enduring monument to vision and hard work, and not replaced for 56 years.

John Conway, pictured with Galen Clark, was the master trail and road builder of Yosemite. In 1875, he engineered the original toll road from the South Fork to Yosemite Valley (Sam Conway Collection.)

Chapter IV

Partnerships

•

Almost before the dust from the July 22nd celebration had settled, Washburn, Chapman, and Coffman put a force of Chinese to work constructing a "large trail" from the far side of the meadow to the Mariposa Grove of Big Trees, a distance of about six miles. "Verily this is a season favorable to the building of new roads and trails in Mariposa County," exulted *Gazette* editor Reynolds. "To say that she is not possessed of men of enterprise and capital would be a terrific falsehood."

In late April, 1876, the entrepreneurs introduced a horse-powered snowplow of their own invention to hasten opening of the road to Yosemite. Chapman was in charge of the firm's stage office and stables at El Capitan meadow in the Valley, while Coffman seems to have been responsible for the Mariposa office and "commodious stable with corral attached" that had been built on Mariposa's main street. Mariposa was a lunch stop for the 25-40 daily passengers who ate at Gallison's Hotel, run by a sister of Jack McCready. Afterward tourists climbed back on the lightly upholstered seats in one of the stages, which had leather springs, flat tops, and open sides, but was still luxurious compared to a "mud wagon" used when the roads were first opened. Because of its versatility, the rough-riding, but indispensable "mud-wagon" has been likened to today's family station wagon. Its four seats were removable so it could be converted into a freight wagon.

". . . we were obliged once more to pack ourselves into the vile van which does duty as a coach," wrote one resigned world-traveler. "They tell us that later in the season, when the roads have been repaired, they will put on good coaches." Although passengers complained of aches and bruises from the jolting vehicles with "angular or knife-board seats," most of them praised the stage drivers. Their hands were skilled, their stories and oaths colorful, and their buttocks seemingly inured to the rides. To a man they were loyal to Henry Washburn who knew, and treated, them well. Their salaries were $40.00 a month for six-to-eight months work, and a few were employed year round. "Kingpin driver" was George Monroe. "His employers say of him that he never met with any accident, never failed to be on time and never cost the company a quarter of a dollar for damages to passengers, horses or vehicles . . ." reported a *Mariposa Gazette*. Monroe's skill, personality, and color, in a country where blacks were a rarity, his comparatively early death, and the fact that Fort Monroe, a stage stop, was named after him, garnered him a disproportionate amount of publicity.

Hi Rapelje, Alex (Gassy) Early and Billy Dowst, were also topnotch drivers. James and Joe Ridgway, Tom and Eddie Gordon (father and son), Henry and Al Skelton (brothers), "Bright" Gillespie, Sam Uren, C.K. Salmon, Jack Ashworth, Henry Hedges, W.J. White, and James Warner are among those who deserve recog-

27

nition. Only one Washburn driver was killed in a stage wreck, but accidents weren't uncommon. As for hold-ups, the scourge of the Sierra, at least six took place en route to the South Fork, all between 1883 and 1911.

Sometime during 1876, a 16-room, single-story lodging house with a New England look to it was built at Big Tree Station. It was named the "Long White." Joseph Shelley, a "mechanic", i.e. carpenter, was the builder. Even with that addition added to the collection of one-story buildings from the Clark era, the Moores were hard put to provide beds, let alone rooms, for travelers. An 1877 inventory shows that there were only 54 beds, including 16 double ones, 8 cots, and 134 blankets to give guests comfort and warmth. Although daytime temperatures could exceed 90°, nights were frosty. Over 1,900 tourists visited the Yosemite Grant in 1876, half or more of which traveled in by the South Fork, primarily during April, May, and June, the months of greatest beauty and water flow. After the 1876 season, "Deacon" and Huldah Moore settled in the infant lumber mill town of Madera (Spanish for lumber), where he ran a store and later served as postmaster and Wells Fargo agent.

That fall, the partners repaid $3,500 dollars, then borrowed $15,450 for which Big Tree Station, its surrounding acreages, improvements, sawmill, and water ditch were mortgaged. Some of that money was spent on the new building, some on the "large trail" to the Big Trees.

On January 1, 1877, an inventory of all Washburn, Chapman, and Coffman's properties was taken. Besides the bedding already noted, there were 138 sheets, 53 bedspreads, 40 wash bowls, 244 towels, 37 chamber pots (valued at $1.00 each), a cooking stove worth $20, a kitchen range and fixtures valued at $200, 9 bread pails, 25 milk pails, and a large assortment of dishes. The only items enumerated even remotely suggesting entertainment were one bookcase, pre-sumably housing books, and 77 large and medium-sized photographs, which were for sale. Guests were expected to amuse themselves by hiking, fishing, or sitting in one of the 68 chairs, admiring the view. From porches, visitors were absorbed by the restful, pastoral beauty of the meadow, heightened by the sounds of river, birds, cows, and, at times, a coyote. Peace was the essential charm, disturbed only briefly by hoofbeats and dust heralding the arrival of a stage.

Among the stables at the Station, Yosemite Valley, Mariposa, and Merced, the firm owned 108 stage horses, 85 saddle horses, and 15 mules valued at $7,275. Seventeen stages, wagons, and buggies, plus a buckboard and three sprinkling carts were listed among rolling stock valued at $5,725. Real estate in Mariposa, Merced, Yosemite Valley, Big Tree Station, and Little Yosemite Valley was evaluated at $30,000.

This meticulous inventory signaled another change of partnership. On March 8, Chapman and Coffman sold their half-interest to Washburn for $21,000, but re-

Albert O. Bruce, another brother-in-law of Washburn's, was a mining engineer who ran the Big Tree Station sawmill. In 1978, a 9,400 foot mountain near Wawona was named for him. (A. W. Hood copy.)

mained his friends and supporters. Coffman bought James Hutchings' livestock and stables in Yosemite Valley and continued in that business until his death in 1898. After 1885, he had George W. Kenney as a partner and built extensive stables called Kenneyville in the upper end of the Valley, where The Ahwahnee Hotel now stands. At times, Coffman represented Washburn in business matters. Chapman's identifi-cation with Yosemite was more tenuous, but he was a Yosemite Valley Commissioner from 1884 until 1888, and Kenneyville's one main road was named Chapman Avenue.

Presumably the firm dissolved because the main objective, the road into Yosemite Valley, had been accomplished, and none of the three was interested in hotelkeeping. Still, Big Tree Station required a keeper, and Washburn acquired one on March 9 when his wife's nephew, John B. Bruce, paid $20,000 for an undivided half of the South Fork property. In a separate agreement, Bruce and the ubiquitous J.J. Cook purchased half-interest in the stage line and stables. In addition, Cook paid Bruce $1,000 for a fourth interest in some of the acreage surrounding Big

Tree Station. Cook was associated with photographer I.W. Taber in San Francisco and kept Big Tree Station supplied with Taber photos to display and sell. Bruce's father, Charles, who had managed Cook's Mariposa drugstore for years, promptly moved to Merced as stage agent.

Johnny Bruce, then 42, was a lively, popular fellow with a host of friends in Merced where he lived with his wife, Catherine Nichols Bruce, 29, and a two-year-old daughter. He "was universally esteemed," the *Merced Star* noted. Soon convivial Bruce was ensconced at Big Tree Station as host, trouble-shooter, and book-keeper, and Washburn could be on the road to drum up trade, buy horses, and other materials. Transportation was the key to the tourist business as good roads, stages, teams and drivers were essential. So was money. Already, Washburn had discovered that road tolls did not equal expenditures. In 1880, for example, $195 was collected in tolls for the use of the South Fork to Yosemite Valley road versus $1,494 expense for clearing snow and trees from it, filling pot holes, repairing washouts, and bridges. On November 1, 1877, Washburn filed incorporation papers for the Yosemite Stage & Turnpike Co. to maintain a freight, express, passenger stage line, and livery busines, from Merced to Big Tree Station, Yosemite Valley, Glacier Point, Nevada Fall, Mariposa Grove of Big Trees, the Fresno Grove, Fresno Flats, and Madera, totaling 165 miles of stage road, 73 of those toll. The inclusion of Glacier Point, Fresno Flats (now Oakhurst), and Madera implied vision, for no roads existed between them in 1877. Capital stock of $25,000 ($10.00 per share) was issued to five directors. Washburn was by far the largest stockholder with 2,300 shares. Four Bay Area businessmen owned 50 shares each. San Francisco was named as the principal place of business, and Washburn appointed superintendent. He so enjoyed the title that he had a rubber stamp made with his name and position and often used it in lieu of signing hotel registers.

Preserved ledgers prove there was profit in the Yosemite Stage & Turnpike business. In fact, it returned far more than did Big Tree Station. The bookkeeping system for the hotel had several income accounts, principally board, bar, laundry, baths, merchandise (sold in the company store), pasturage, stabling, lumber or saw mill, and building. Not surprisingly, the bar account was lengthy; the bath one, brief. Primary expenses were wages and food, but produce gardens, dairy cows, beef, pork, and chicken raised on the ranch helped cut costs. Tom Hambridge, known as Indian Tom, supplied the hotel with fish caught in the South Fork, and Pleasant R. Gipson, a nearby farmer, provided potatoes and apples.

Frequently-changed, six horse teams were required to haul heavy freight wagons over the Chowchilla Mountain Road. (Sam Conway Collection.)

Convivial Johnny Bruce, an able and well-liked innkeeper, was an excellent partner for Henry Washburn. (YNP Collection.)

Ah Tom, Henry, Ah Jim and Ah Cook presided in the kitchen while other Chinese worked in the laundry. Henry was the highest paid, at $100 a month. "Indian Tom" caught fish, gardened, cut wood, hay, and ice, and sometimes did laundry work. Later "Indian Jim" received wages for similar jobs.

By then only a handful of Indians were living at Wawona, the area their ancestors had called Pallah-chun, "a good place to stop." Their camp was a ramshackle, half-umacha, half-house settlement on the far side of the river from the hotel. White man's culture, economy, and liquor had ended their traditional, independent way of life. Unable to pronounce Indian names, the white man demeaned them with graphic substitutes such as Bush-head Tom, Short and Dirty, and One-eyed Bullock. Partial integration was inevitable, but justice was rarely on the Indians' side. Witnesses saw a white man murder "Bush-head" Tom Hambridge in 1889. A trial was held in Mariposa, but the case was dismissed on "insufficient evidence."

So, sadly, "a good place to stop" was a good place to stay for the white pioneers, but not the natives.

Only a handful of women were on the staff in the late 1870's when the pay for a chambermaid or waitress was $40 per month. Chief among them was Azelia Van Campen Bruce, sister-in-law to Jean Washburn, who did maid work, sewing, and might have been called housekeeper. Her husband, Al Bruce, was a mining engineer and jack-of-all trades who ran and improved the water-powered saw mill. His salary was the same as his wife's, an oddity in those days of inequality. Board for the help was $20 a month, and they spent most of the remainder in the store and bar. Barkeeper at $25 a month was Billy Nichols, Bruce's brother-in-law.

Several men who did nothing but road repair at $1.34 per day boarded at the Station, as did a milkman, a clerk, and stage drivers who were pasing through. Excepting the chefs, the bosses — Bruce, Washburn, and J.J. Cook — were the highest paid with a take of around $100 a month each.

From Irish chambermaid to Chinese chef, milkman to manager, the heterogeneous staff united talents and skills to transport, feed, and house guests. Constance F. Gordon-Cumming, a cultured Scotswoman, commented approvingly on them and Big Tree Station in an April, 1878, letter, later published in her book, *Granite Crags*. After a wearying, but nonetheless "magnificent drive" from Mariposa, she found "comfortable quarters awaiting us here in a cosy group of one-storied houses, with separate cottages for bedrooms — everything clean and pleasant, kind people, and none of the stiffness and insouciance of a regular hotel . . ."

Her letter bore a Big Tree Station postmark, for the place had been established as a California post office on April 18 with Johnny Bruce as postmaster.

In August, Collis P. Huntington, president of the Southern Pacific Railroad, who had at least an advisory influence on Washburn, spent a night at Big Tree Station where he was treated as royally as could be managed. By then Washburn and Bruce were financing a fifteen-mile road from the South Fork to Fresno Flats, and a road from Fresno Flats to Madera, a Southern Pacific stop, was being surveyed.

Neither Washburn nor his predecessor Clark had ever been happy with the support given them by Mariposa County. Year after year, their appropriations had been virtually non-existent, yet Clark, Washburn, and various partners had brought a great deal of money into the county, and their needs for employees, food, hay, and livestock had benefited many residents. Every stage passenger who stopped in Mariposa meant money in restaurant, hotel, and shop tills, yet county supervisors would not finance adequate roads or maintain existing ones. Venturesome, aggressive Washburn had looked afield, and the flattish field toward Madera looked good.

The new route was about six miles longer than the Merced-South Fork road, but its grades were easier, and construction and maintenance less costly. A branch railroad line to a point closer to Big Tree Station was a possibility that Washburn must have discussed with C.P. Huntington. Although undocumented, ties with the Southern Pacific were close even then.

Directing the road construction was Washburn's major project in 1878, but a family reunion was an exciting highlight. His brothers, John, then 40, and Edward, 43, journeyed to California in April, 1878.

*Henry Washburn, the transportation king of the Sierra, was
an aggressive businessman, yet loyal and overwhelmingly
generous. He saw Yosemite Valley for the first time in 1859.
(I. W. Taber photograph; YNP Collection.)*

Washburn and Bruce added the building at the right, known today as the Clark Cottage, in 1876. Of the buildings shown, it was the sole survivor of the 1878 fire. (WWH Collection.)

John's recent life had been tragic for his young son had died in 1874, and his wife had succumbed to consumption in 1875. It seems certain that Henry had pressed the bereft widower, and bachelor Ed, to move to California where temperate climate, beauty, and jobs awaited them.

Like brother Henry, John resembled famed Ulysses Grant. He was a stalwart, good-looking man of 5' 10" with blue eyes, brown hair, beard, and moustache. From his first appearance in Yosemite, he was regarded highly, partly because of his unfailingly courteous personality as well as his unmarried state. In 1881 it was emblazoned in *Mariposa Gazette* print, that he was "single, good-looking and it's a wonder some young lady hasn't pushed him off some of these high cliffs 'ere this and made a 'mash' of him."

John's exact position with Washburn and Bruce in the early years is not known, but he may have worked in the Yosemite Valley office as a booking agent. In frequent registrations at La Casa Nevada, however, he gave Big Tree Station as his residence, as he did when he became a Mariposa County voter on March 22, 1879.

Edward's beard and moustache were less luxuriant than those of his brothers, and he was leaner. He stood 5' 10" with blue eyes, brown hair, and neat features. Mild-mannered, he remained a confirmed, precise bachelor who never uttered so much as a hearty "Damn". When provoked, he would exclaim softly, but definitely, "Oh, pshaw!"

Henry had long wanted Ed to take over as stage agent in Merced. He soon had the books balanced perfectly and was efficient at arranging transportation for people and freight. Naturally, he visited Big Tree Station and Yosemite Valley, but his home and job were in Merced.

According to a Merced newspaper, travel was "brisk" at Big Tree Station during October, 1878, with tourists arriving even in mid-November. Men were still at work finishing the South Fork-Fresno Flats section as well as the road to the Mariposa Grove. Both Washburn and Bruce were jubilant at the prospects of increased visitation over the new route the following spring.

All was well until Saturday, November 29, when flames spurted from a kitchen stovepipe and "devoured large buildings and their valuable contents." Tom Gordon and a large crew of Chinese laborers saw the billowing smoke from the Big Tree road and rushed down, convinced that the stable barn was burning. By the time they arrived, however, that barn was one of the few surviving buildings, whereas the laundry and four small row (bedroom) buildings were only smoking ruins.

CHAPTER V

Big Tree Station

•

A jay scolded from the singed bough of a ponderosa pine as Washburn and Bruce surveyed the ashes of buildings and furnishings. Only the two-year-old Long White building and the stables remained from the complex of makeshift, pioneer structures. They estimated their financial loss at $10,000; a month later the Mariposa County tax assessor reduced official valuation from $14,460 to $8,330. Necessity gave the resolute partners the opportunity to build more substantial, suitable hotel facilities.

Within a week of the fire, they hired Joseph Shelly, builder of the Long White, and staked out a large building that was to have two stories. "Four large teams left Merced one day during the week for Big Tree Station," reported the December 21, *San Joaquin Valley Argus,* "heavily loaded with materials for the rebuilding of the hotel, lately destroyed by fire. The proprietors, Messers Washburn and Bruce, have also set up a planing machine of 16 horse power."

A week later the *Gazette* stated that the new building was progressing rapidly even though ice was thick. Winter must have slowed construciton, but the March 8, 1879, *Gazette* recorded that "The large building now in the course of building at Big Tree Station is said to be 140 by 32 feet, two stories high, and, when completed, will be the grandest hotel in the mountains of California." As befitting a grand hotel, the new unit had a lobby, sitting room, dining room, and office on the lower floor, and 25 small guest rooms above.

Upstairs and down, covered porches encircled the building.

Ledger accounts show that Shelly, Al Bruce, and W.R. Knight, the carpenters, were paid $764, $504 and $230 respectively, while J.S. French was paid $130 for making 20,775 shakes. The new hotel was ready for business on Tuesday, April 1 when 19 tourists, the first of the season, arrived, although according to the *Gazette,* Shelly was still "engaged at carpentering and building" in late June.

No longer was a "saddle train" needed to carry sightseers to the Mariposa Grove; instead they could travel by stage over the new road, which had cost the Yosemite Stage and Turnpike Company $1,250 to construct. Roadbuilder Washburn described it as "exceedingly meandering in character . . ."

As might be expected, Henry Washburn was aboard the first stage to arrive from Mariposa and greeted the first one that came in on the new road from Madera. Beginning April 1, daily stages left Madera at 6 a.m., and arrived at Big Tree Station about twelve hours later. At first six-horse teams were used, but they had a hard time negotiating the sharp turns, so four horses were put on in the mountains. When Nevada-raised mustangs proved too small for the hauls, Washburn bought larger horses from Miller and Lux, whose vast land holdings dominated the San Joaquin Valley. Because horses had to be changed every four to eight miles, depending on the terrain, it took 72 horses to

Upon completion in the spring of 1879, the 32 by 140 foot, two story building was acclaimed "the grandest hotel in the mountains of California." Wawona Dome in background. (George Fiske photograph; SS Collection.)

haul each stage from Madera to Yosemite Valley.

Round trip fare was $45 and as many as 40 passengers, on four stages, came in each day. About half of these travelers were from other countries, and perhaps a quarter from Eastern states. Californians were too busy settling in, and making a living, to vacation.

Immediately after his unhappy second term as president, Civil War hero Ulysses S. Grant began a well-publicized round-the-world trip. Toward its end, he and his party of ten visited Yosemite. When Grant emerged from his palace car in Madera at 6 a.m. on October 2, 1879, Henry Washburn and ace driver Hi Rapelje awaited him with a six-horse, eleven-passenger stage. During most of the twelve-hour ride, Grant "occupied the seat of honor with the driver." Even though it was dark, Indians literally kept their ears to the ground so as to be the first to announce the stage's approach. Big Tree Station guests and campers, and the Mariposa Brass Band greeted Grant with acclaim and "Hail To The Chief." "The grounds were set with evergreens, and in the center an improvised fountain threw a stream of water forty feet in height,"

reported the *San Francisco Chronicle* . . . "So much road dust covered the General that he looked as if he had been engaged in the most hotly contested battle of the wilderness."

Naturally the new building had been decorated inside by the Bruces and Jean Bruce Washburn. Later, she wrote that she "was charmed with the President & wife. Put on no airs but chatted with me pleasantly as if my friends . . . They are the sweetest, most unassuming couple I ever met to be so high in position."

Next day, driven by George Monroe and accompanied by the band, the party traveled to Yosemite Valley where they stayed at Barnard's Hotel. The story goes that Mrs. Leidig, co-owner of a rival hotel, sent her sons up to see the ex-president. Upon return, one said disgustedly, "All we saw was Mr. Washburn and some other men sitting on the porch." To them the two were indistinguishable.

Monroe piloted the party to, and through, the Mariposa Grove on October 5. They spent that night at Big Tree Station where charge for room and board was $4.00 for each of the eleven. Billy Dowst was the driver for the trip to Merced via the Chowchilla

Mountain Road to Mariposa where the party stopped for lunch at Gallison's Hotel. Mariposans gave Grant a tumultuous welcome, and *Gazette* editor Reynolds wrote: "Mr. Henry Washburn deserves the thanks of our entire community for bringing General Grant over this route."

In contrast to the press coverage of every detail of Grant's visit to Yosemite, that of President Rutherford B. Hayes in October, 1880, received almost no attention, except the *Fresno Expositer* revealed that by pre-arrangement 500 of Reese's best Havanas awaited him in Madera "for the use of himself and party on the trip to Yo Semite."

No stage was greeted more eagerly than one from Merced which arrived at the Station sometime in June, 1879, for Johnny's Bruce's wife, Catherine, and baby were aboard it. She had gone to Merced for the birth of her third child, and Bruce was hoping for a boy "because in his genealogy each alternate generation had had a John Bruce and then a Charles Bruce." That was the memory of the baby who long after she grew up recorded, "As the stage landed at the platform my sister, Fannie, cried out, 'Oh, Daddy, it's a girl and it's a redhead.' So my father had to be satisfied with a Charlotte instead of a Charles."

Bruce was undaunted and as full of ideas as his partner. In 1881, for example, he promoted the "first show ever at Big Tree Station," pushed a road to Signal Peak, 7,800 feet high, and suggested damming Big Creek to make a 100-acre pond that would provide ice skating in winter and ice for summer use. Not only was he a good hotel manager, but he managed his personal finances well. He had bought 2,500 shares of the Yosemite Stage & Turnpike Co., valued at $10 per share, owned one-fourth interest in buildings, furnishings, and lands adjoining the Station, and had loaned partner Washburn $443 at 1 percent interest a month.

After August 27, 1881, the partners ran a weekly ad in the *Gazette* for their new sawmill that offered "dressed and ready for use" lumber, "rustic weather boarding," and seasoned "sugar-pine planks" in exchange for "BARLEY, WHEAT, CORN, FLOUR, POULTRY, EGGS, SHEEP-CATTLE (and coin) at Farm Market prices."

That same year, Washburn and Bruce paid Otis, Ben, and Lyman Scribner $75 to enlarge a natural cavity in a giant Sequoia that blocked a new road they were building from the Lower Grove through the Upper one. They cut an eight-foot-wide, 26-foot long "tunnel," which was finished early in August. A stage driver and a Knights Templar from Philadelphia were the first to drive through the tree. They were followed by thousands of people on foot, horseback, stage, and in time, automobile, for the Wawona Tree quickly became a tourist mecca, immortalized in pictures seen in books and homes all over the world. Eventually, a man did nothing but photograph people and vehicles

In 1882, meticulous Edward Washburn settled in as book-keeper at Big Tree Station. (I. W. Taber photograph; WWH Collection.)

emerging from the tree for later sale to the delighted subjects.

Although John Bruce had suffered a slight stroke early in 1881, it didn't stop him from renewing his bond as postmaster, superintending the "building of a new house at Big Tree Station," and enlarging the sawmill. After the tourist season ended, however, he planned to take a railroad trip through Southern California to recuperate, but he was back soon after New Year's, 1882. On March 2, while leaning over to tie his shoes, he died from a stroke. A crowd of friends and business associates attended graveside services in Merced. Because only Bruce and Henry Washburn knew the combination of the safe at the hotel, Catherine Bruce could not retrieve his will until Washburn came up in late April. After probate was concluded, in October, 1883, he paid her $5,000 for his former partner's interest.

Five years later Catherine died, and big-hearted Henry Washburn gathered up the three girls to take to his wife, their aunt, in San Francisco. Mrs. Washburn's welcome was reluctant for her affections were reserved for her poetry and teenage daughter Jeannie, but the orphans had a home. Big Tree Station, where they still spent summers, remained their favorite place, and "Uncle Henry" their favorite relative. His home and voting registration were there, though he was in and

Vegetables, fruit, berries, chicken, hogs, sheep, and cattle were raised to supply hotel guests with tasty meals. (WWH Collection.)

After 1878, tourists could travel by stage to the Mariposa Grove over a new road which Washburn described as "exceedingly meandering in character." (SS Collection.)

From a nearby peak, the new hotel was almost hidden by the forest. (Putnam and Valentine; SS Collection.)

out of a house on Fillmore Street in the City to which the family had moved from Merced. In addition, he maintained a suite in the Palace Hotel where business deals, politics, and poker took place.

Bruce's death was a great loss for he had been an able and affable partner, hotel manager, and bookkeeper. Temperamentally, John Washburn, whom Bruce had trained, was well-suited to be manager for he was courteous and friendly, kept a sharp eye on guest comfort and the staff who provided it, but was not adept with accounts. Henry observed the situation, and in April, 1883, transferred brother Ed from the Merced office to the South Fork as bookkeeper. Thus the three brothers began to work in what became a smooth-operating team, although it was not formalized as such for years.

J.J. Cook remained almost a silent partner, but from a powerful new vantage point, Yosemite Valley, where he managed the former Black's Hotel from about 1883 until 1887. Naturally, he had fingers in every political pie, which strengthened Washburn's already strong alliances with the Yosemite Valley Commissioners and the concessionaires in their charge. Cook's son, Jay Bruce Cook, was also active in the Valley hotel.

In 1883 reliable, efficient John Conway was pushing the work on 14 miles of road from Chinquapin to Glacier Point. A total of $8,000 was spent on it by the Yosemite Stage & Turnpike Co., and it was immediately popular with tourists after its opening about June 1.

By mid-May men were stringing telegraph lines to Big Tree Station, connecting it with Yosemite Valley, Mariposa, Merced, and Madera, a step backed and welcomed by Henry Washburn. After that, rooms could be reserved by wire, and the staff had some knowledge of how many stages and passengers could be expected each day.

Early in August a stage approaching Grouse Creek was stopped by two men afoot who pointed shotguns at the six passengers, forcing them to hand over $2,000 in money and jewelry. That was the first hold-up of a Washburn stage, but Henry was relieved that the robbers hadn't waited for the second stage, as it was carrying fourteen passengers and the Wells Fargo express box. A reward of $250 was offered by the company, but the robbers were never apprehended.

A general store, blacksmith shop, wagon shop, and a saloon had been built close to Big Tree Station so it resembled a village. As a hotel, it had status and no more enthusiastic supporter than editor Reynolds of the *Mariposa Gazette,* who boosted it as one of the best in California, ". . . vegetables, eggs, apples, oranges, strawberries, everything in the front line that can be found in the markets of the state can be found there." Everything he listed except oranges was grown at the increasingly popular resort. Much of the meadow had been fenced and cross-fenced to corral cattle, horses, sheep, and hogs. Hay, barley, and potatoes grew in fields, but the thrifty farm appearance was still bounded by thick forest, thrusting mountains, and bald granite domes. From a pioneer stage stop with a primitive inn, Big Tree Station had become a partly self-sustaining mountain resort of importance and appeal.

In August, 1881 two brothers were paid $75 to enlarge a natural cavity in the Wawona Tree to a nine foot high, eight foot wide, 26 foot long "tunnel". It was an instant magnet for visitors who continued to pass through, and photograph it, until the tree fell early in 1969. (Putnam and Valentine, 1901; SS Collection.)

CHAPTER VI

Wawona

•

In 1882, poetical Jean Bruce Washburn, a long-time observer of Indian lore, suggested the euphonious Indian word, Wah-wo-nah, meaning big tree*, as a more fitting name than Big Tree Station for the hotel complex. By September 10, 1882, her name was official for the hotel and post-office. Local residents were less acceptive of the new title as proved by the 1884 Maripos County Great Register. Of the 21 men registering as voters in Wawona, 19 gave Big Tree Station as residence, while only two acknowledged Wawona. Within a few years, however, Wawona adhered to the entire area.

Thomas Hill was among the registrants. Englishborn Hill was already famed for his paintings of Yosemite and other scenic wonderlands. In 1883 he had had a studio erected in Yosemite Valley, but a gale literally blew it off its foundations, so he moved to Wawona where he was welcomed by the Washburns as a cultural asset.

John Washburn was particularly hospitable because he was courting Estella Louise Hill, one of the artist's nine children. Tiny, pretty, talented Estella, 20, was vivacious and social, and used to the cosmopolitan society of her parents' Oakland home. Despite the age disparity, she was in love with the gentle but stalwart hotelkeeper. Their April, 1885, marriage took place in Oakland, and they honeymooned at the Del Monte Hotel, but thereafter Wawona was their beloved home.

They moved into the only guest rooms downstairs in the main building, and Estella's personality, singing, and piano playing soon endeared her to staff and guests alike. Their only child, Clarence Arthur, was born January 18, 1886, in Oakland, and brought to Wawona where he was royally welcomed by father and uncles in April.

"Grandpa" Hill lived upstairs in rooms 10 and 11, but spent most of his time in a three-room studio built for him on the grounds in 1886. Its interior was lavishly embellished with his landscapes, as well as bear skins, Indian baskets, deer antlers, animal pelts, a hornet's nest, and other natural artifacts. A billiard table furnished one side room while Hill's easel was dominant in the other. Visitors were welcome, and marvelled at his ability to smoke a cigar, carry on conversation, and paint all at the same time. Of course, they bought many of his fine paintings, and they were shipped, in boxes he made himself, all over the world since many guests were foreigners.

Hill was short and slight, but a prodigious worker with brush, hammer, and saw. He made his own canvas stretchers, built a rustic walkway, benches, and two rowboats for Stella Lake. Although constructed

---

*Years later Indian authority Stephen Power stated that the Sequoia was so sacred to the Indians they called it "wah-woh-nau," a word, he said, "formed in imitation of the hoot of an owl, which is the guardian spirit and diety of this great monarch of the forest."

Stella Lake, named for Estella Washburn, was popular with hotel guests (WWH Collection.)

Engaging Estella Hill was only 20 when she married John Washburn, 47, in 1885, but they were a compatible and devoted couple. (WWH Collection.)

as an ice pond to supply the hotel, the lake, named after Estella Washburn, quickly became a popular recreational spot for guests.

In 1886 Hill's romanticized sketch of the hotel complex, showing non-existent fences, and a spouting fountain, appeared in James Hutchings' book *In The Heart of the Sierras*. Within a year or two, two fountains, probably inspired by the pictures, were installed; a big one in front of the main hotel, and a small one by Hill's Studio. In it he kept and fed live trout he had caught. In his early years, Hill had been an ardent and successful fisherman, but later recoiled from killing anything.

Son Edward, a much lesser painter, and his pretty wife Willeta were often at Wawona. After their divorce, she became Hill's devoted receptionist. He allowed her and Estella to sell pressed and mounted wildflowers in his studio, but nothing esle was sold there except his paintings.

The 1880's and '90's were years of success, variety, and interest at the hotel. A third guest cottage, the Little White, had been added to the row in 1884, and its three high-ceiled rooms were usually rented to families. All the buildings were resplendently white, and had a look of permanence. Charlotte Bruce, who was raised there, wrote later, that a "Periclean age" endured ". . . because here was a civilization second to none. I can remember a night at Wawona when the logs were blazing in the office and there were gathered there a United States Senator, stage drivers, Indian guides, an East Indian prince, and various Army officers."

Among the prominent visitors were John Ruskin, U.S. Grant, Lily Langtry, Bernard Baruch, Diamond Jim Brady, William Jennings Bryan, William Harrison, and many others.

Bombastic, spellbinder William Jennings Bryan made a tremendous hit with staff and residents. Almost before the stage stopped, he jumped off and began shaking hands with everyone from chambermaids to Chinese cooks. That night he made a talk at the dance hall, which was packed with local Democrats and a few avid Republicans such as Azelia Bruce. She was so carried away by Bryan's oratory that when he concluded talking, she climbed up on the platform, threw her arms around him and kissed him.

"I think Mr. Blyan velly good man," was the sober pronouncement of Ah You. Henry Washburn had plucked Ah You from a miner's job at Hite's Cove in the early 1880's, and before long he was renowned for his culinary skills in the hotel kitchen. In 1890 ex-president William H. Harrison complimented Ah You on his fried chicken; his hearty handshake made the diminutive Cantonese quiver.

"Wawona was famous for its food," Charlotte Bruce recorded. "It had its own garden from which all the vegetables came; they killed their own meat; they fished out of the rivers. Milk came from their own cows, and,

Hill's Studio was a gathering place for guests who watched the genial artist paint, and sometimes purchased his fine landscapes of Yosemite. (YNP Collection.)

in game season, there was quail on toast and venison. A typical Wawona breakfast consisted of fruit in season, beefsteak, ham and eggs, trout, hot cakes, and cornbread with homemade preserves. This was not to give a diner a choice, but to be eaten in its entirety. The rate for room and board was $4.00 a day.

Charlotte also recalled that a bulletin board was a feature of the front porch of the main building. If notables were coming, their names were always posted. ". . . and I remember going to see what was posted when we children arrived for the summer. . . . 'A.H. Washburn, 5 kids and a box of dogs.'" "Uncle Harry" was their adored second father, but they loved "Uncle John," little "Cousin Clarence," and crusty "Uncle Ed" as well, and enlivened, if not disrupted, the operation of the hotel.

As noted earlier, that operation was remarkably cohesive, as was the relationship of the three brothers. Although he was uncompromisingly correct, "Uncle Ed" was a soft touch, as Fannie, Alice, and Charlotte Bruce knew. Ed kept in touch with Julius, who still ran the Washburn farm in Vermont, and often enclosed a check for his seven children.

While Ed labored behind the scenes, John was highly visible and approachable to guests, who came to him

Thomas Hill was the resident artist at the Wawona Hotel from 1884 until his death in 1908. (I.W. Taber photograph; WWH Collection.)

Ah You's pies were the pride of Wawona where he presided over the hotel kitchen for 47 years. Theodore Roosevelt, and local children were among his many admirers. (YNP Collections.)

Despite his grave appearance, handsome John Washburn had a good sense of humor. (I.W. Taber photograph; WWH Collection.)

42

with complaints, problems, and praise. Customarily soft-spoken, he could solve most difficulties, but sometimes expressed displeasure. After a woman complained at length that the accomodations were poor, roads rough, stages crowded and small, horses wild, and the driver too young to handle them, John seated her in a departing stage with his usual courtesy. "Goodbye, madame," he said quietly. "If you are as disagreeable at home as you have been here, I feel sorry for your neighbors."

"Mrs. John," as Estella Washburn was called, used her green thumb in growing flowers, especially roses and petunias, but also loved wildflowers. She made most of Clarence's clothes, and condoned his lighthearted mischief. Like his father, Clarence was full of fun. As she said, the two of them led her to "expect the best, prepare for the worst, and make the most of what comes." Clarence was here, there, and everywhere, pulling his little wagon, soliciting goodies from Ah You, riding horseback, and learning to fish. Grandpa Hill painted Clarence's portrait in which he looked neat and faintly cherubic, an appearance contrary to his robust, outdoor life. When William Sell came to the hotel as a telegrapher about 1890, Clarence acquired an inseparable buddy in Will Sell, Jr.

"Mrs. Henry" was not often at Wawona, preferring San Francisco culture. Probably because her stays were transitory, she and her family had the worst rooms in the place, upstairs in the back. While there, in the opinion of contemporaries, she dominated everyone except her husband.

No one told Henry Washburn what to do for he was a dominant, yet not dominating, person. As transportation king of Yosemite, in company with his old associate, E. W. Chapman and other Maderans, Henry had incorporated a railroad company in 1881 with the ambitious intention of building a trans-Sierra line across the mountains to Mammoth area mines. A terminus near Fresno Flats was to serve Yosemite, but the pretentious scheme floundered. Still, Henry wanted rails to come closer than Madera, and the rainy winter of 1885-86 advanced his cause. "If we expect to move tourists into Yosemite this spring, we will have to start from some point other than Madera," he told Southern Pacific officials, "because the rains have been so heavy there will be no bottom between Madera and the foothills."

Soon Berenda, seven miles north of Madera, was selected as the new rail terminus, and tracks were laid by Chinamen from there to a point 22 miles away on an oak-dotted flat beyond which foothills rose abruptly. As soon as the terminal was known, enterprising men laid out a townsite, and began building. When the first passenger train huffed in on May 14, 1886, a tent hotel was already open, and other buildings under construction. Washburn had corrals, barns, and cottages built for the Yosemite Stage & Turnpike Co. operations. Washburn would have been

For the mountains ring with laughter. "While folks gather like bees/To sip the social honey/And picnic neath the trees," wrote Estella Washburn who thought Wawona was "sublime." (WWH Collection.)

an appropriate name for the settlement, but it was called Raymond in honor of Walter Raymond of the popular Raymond-Whitcomb Boston-to-Boston tours. Side trips to Yosemite were a specialty that benefited the Southern Pacific, the Washburns, and Yosemite Valley concessionaires.

Daily trains, one from Los Angeles and the other from San Francisco, brought passengers to Raymond where they spent a night before boarding shiny eight- or eleven-passenger stages pulled by well-groomed horses commanded by trusted stagedrivers. Ultimately, four hotels served tourists. In 1890 the Yosemite Stage & Turnpike Co. built a large one, and Washburn installed Isabella and George Leidig, Yosemite Valley pioneers, as hosts.

Miami Mills was one of the many stage stops where horses were changed. (Putnam & Valentine, 1901; SS Collection.)

After 1890, Awhawnee was the lunch stop. In partnership with Henry Washburn, William Sell had bought an old ranch, renamed it, and built a charming, two-storied home with a large dining room and wide porches. "A refreshing rest and an excellent midday meal," was obtainable there, according to Hutchings' *Yosemite and The Big Trees* guidebook of 1895. Will and Etta Grace Sell were the hospitable proprietors.

In July, 1887, Washburn decided to participate in Fourth of July festivities in Yosemite Valley. When he stopped his buggy for a fresh team in Chinquapin, he discovered that none of the horses had been fed or harnessed, and the hostler, Johnson Ridley, was drunk. Holiday or not, Washburn would not tolerate incompetence, fired Johnson, and ordered him to leave on the next stage.

Hours later, as Washburn was finishing a dram of whiskey in Barnard's Hotel, Ridley stepped in and shot the glass from his hand. Washburn was unhurt, and the assailant quickly pinioned by other men in the bar. After his formal arrest, Ridley revealed that his real name was Patrick Connor. In August he was tried in the county courthouse for assault with intent to commit murder.

After his jury conviction of guilty, the judge asked Connor if he had anything to say for himself. "Yes," he exclaimed, "as soon as I get out, I will shoot you, Henry Washburn, on sight!"

A week later, the judge sentenced Connor to fourteen years in San Quentin. Washburn, who merited the loyal allegiance of a hundred or more employees and a host of friends, was only temporarily disconcerted by the threat. But he never forgot it.

CHAPTER VII

Mountaineers

•

Besides the dominant Washburn triumvirate, the Wawona area abounded with individuals who matched the granite domes with toughness and, in varied ways, contributed to the function of hotel operations. One of the most picturesque was lanky, gaunt Pleasant Reynolds Gipson, a roughhewn native of Tennessee who had a beaky nose, piercing black eyes, gray hair, and a face-enveloping beard. Gipson, an unsuccessful miner, developed apple orchards on a sidehill ranch, bisected by the Chowchilla Mountain road west of Wawona. He sold apples and potatoes to the hotel; e.g. Washburn and Bruce paid him $3.54 for 118 pounds of potatoes in September, 1878. At the same time he owed them $9.13 for whiskey. When well lubricated, he would demand an audience of ladies to hear him croon "The Crow is a Pretty Bird," and "Sugar's sweet and so is honey, but my sweetheart is sweet as any."

In 1903, when he was 82, he sold his 80 acres to the Madera Sugar Pine Company for $900 then left the area. Last, misspelled words from Gipson came to Edward Washburn from McKinney, Texas, in September, 1903. Gipson's spelling was not even phonetic, e.g. "hawtell" for hotel, but he was "right side up," and his folks were "doeing well."

Yosemite guide Nathan Bennett Phillips, known to all as "Pike," was even more colorful then old man Gipson, for Pike told tall tales that expanded with each telling. There was the story about a bear who chased Pike out on a limb of a lofty pine, only to be routed by the mountaineer's growl of "Get back you fool or we'll both be killed!" Another time a bear was ready to crush him with a bear hug, so "I turned around right quick, shoved my arm down the bear's throat, grabbed his tail and turned him inside out." While visiting San Francisco's labyrinthian Palace Hotel, Pike requested a hatchet so "I can blaze a trail out of here." When asked why he spoke in a whisper, he answered that he had lost his voice "telling lies to the tourists." His hoarse, guttural whisper was perfectly distinct. When questioned as to how long he had lived in Yosemite Valley, his reply was, "Ever since they were hauling in the dirt to build it." In contrast, when asked the age of one of the cliffs, he muttered, "Don't know — it was here when I got here."

How Pike "got here," from where, and his early life were a mystery until September, 1978, when the author, while preparing these pages, received a surprising long-distance call from Pike's great-great nephew, Cliff Craker. He sent copies of letters about and from his colorful ancestor, plus factual family background that documents this account.

Pike, or Nathan Bennett Phillips, was born in Bedford County, Tennessee, in 1838, the son of Elzada and Samuel Phillips. In 1840, the family moved to a farm near Marionville, Missouri, which is still owned by Craker's mother. At 21, Pike, a strong, solidly-built fellow, left home for California where he prospected for gold in the Coulterville-Bull Creek area,

45 miles west of Yosemite Valley. "You know I have formed a taste for frontier life," he wrote years later, "& am never so happy as when I am exploring some new country." His explorations took him to Oregon and Arizona, included a "sweetheart" who died, and a butcher business in which he lost $1,500. Once, 12 years passed between his letters, so his mother feared him dead. In July, 1876, an ex-Missourian named Cassidy found the "strangely wild" prodigal son herding ponies in Yosemite Valley, berated him for not "writing to your poor old Ma," then wrote her at length himself. Cassidy revealed that spirits literally were Pike's downfall.

After the lectures, Pike kept in infrequent touch with his mother, boasting of his hunting and mule train. In 1884, he was hired by the Washburns as a butcher, and later worked on their road crew, drove stage, spliced rattlesnake rattles together to make long strings to sell credulous tourists, played a mean fiddle, and served as an able, amusing tourist guide.

In August, 1894, Pike took young Bert Bruce fishing, and spent most of a day wading in the South Fork. That prolonged exposure reportedly caused dropsy. It seems likely that he already had heart failure, complicated, or even caused by his heavy drinking, and the stress of exposure heightened it. After weeks of illness, during which the Washburns provided him with a bed and food, Pike died on October 30. Ed Washburn requested an inquest, so a jury of residents was impanelled and decided death had been caused by "neuralgia of the heart." A doctor might have called it heart failure. Pike had been destitute, but the Washburns took care of their own. Mr. John furnished a suit, and a carpenter and a painter prepared a handsome coffin. Burial was in the small Wawona Cemetery, and Hattie Bruce said that years later an Englishwoman Pike had befriended paid for a headstone.

Another local mountaineer named Jim Duncan was a legendary hunter from the late 1850's on. At first, he confided to John Muir, he had been "mortally afraid of bear, but after killing a half dozen he began to keep count of his victims, and . . . wanted to kill an even hundred."

James Hayden Duncan had been born in Wisconsin in 1835. As a young man he traveled to California where he prospected, owned a quartz mill, raised stock, hunted, and guided geologists Clarence King and J.T. Gardiner on surveying trips. While he was herding hogs near the South Fork in 1857, molesting bears prompted him to engage in hunting as a career. Meat and skins were marketable. Around 1870 he built a log cabin with a large rock fireplace on the shore of Crescent Lake 16 miles east of Wawona. His only "neighbors" were stockman Bob Wellman and his wife, who spent summers in the 7,000 foot elevation area.

"On my excursions," Muir recorded in his *Our National Parks* book, "I occasionally passed by his

A dog and a pipe were Pleasant Gipson's companions on his ranch when photographer A.C. Vroman took his picture in 1901. (Pasadena Public Library; A.W. Hood copy.)

(Duncan's) cabin. It was full of meat and skins hung in bundles from the rafters, and the ground around it was strewn with bones and hair, infinitely less tidy than a bear's den." In 1875 Muir noted 49 notches on a timber, one for each bear Duncan had killed. On one gory day, he slaughtered five.

Besides hunting, and guiding tourists into the back country, Duncan raised horses, some of which he sold to Henry Washburn. In 1887, he was on the jury that found Washburn's assailant guilty. Much of the venison on the hotel menu was supplied by the indefatigable hunter. Grizzly bears were rare, but in October, 1887, Wellman persuaded Duncan to help him kill one who was after his cattle. "Well, Bob," Duncan told his companion, as they climbed onto a platform for the fourth night's watch, "of all the foolish things I've done in my life, I think this is the silliest."

He felt differently after the grizzly was dead, and he and Wellman won acclaim all over Mariposa County. Thomas Hill was so enthusiastic, he bought the skin to hang in his studio, and then painted, "The Grizzly Bear Hunters." After Hill's death, Estella Hill Washburn sold the skin to the Zoology Department of the University of California where it is still preserved. Although the story of the great, and probably last, grizzly grew, the skin, after drying and tanning, shrank from ten to seven-and-a-half feet in length.

Duncan's bear kill totaled somewhere between 80 and 90 before he died near Sacramento on October 3, 1898, of malarial fever — killed by a bug rather than a bear!

Stephen Mandeville Cunningham, native of New York, was an enterprising, early pioneer in Yosemite Valley; in fact, in 1857, he was the first white man to spend winter months there. Subsequently, he built trails, ran a hotel, improved a land claim in the Valley, mined, taught school, and served in the Union Army in California during the Civil War. His popularity was enough that he was named Grand Marshall of the 1875 celebration for the opening of the Wawona Road.

Cunningham's association with Wawona began when he was appointed Guardian of the Mariposa Grove in 1882. That position entailed maintaining trails and roads, fighting fires, and informing the traveling public about the peculiarities of the Sequoias. Many times forest fires, usually caused by lightning, threatened the trees, and he sent word to Henry Washburn who brought a force of men to subdue flames and dig ditches around the endangered trees.

During tourist season, Cunningham lived in a small cabin Clark had built in the Upper Grove, but spent winters in his homestead cabin on the South Fork. Both there and in the hollow "room" of the Stable Tree, he made wood curios out of dead Sequoia wood. As his salary was small and paid irregularly (if at all) by the State Legislature, Cunningham's income depended on road work for the Yosemite Stage & Turnpike Co., and sales of curios.

He was ingenious, amusing, educated, "keenly alive to the poetry of his surroundings," according to an 1889 book, yet a squaw man in the opinion of several

Steve Cunningham was a pioneer in Yosemite Valley before he was appointed Guardian of the Mariposa Grove. (YNP Collection.)

contemporaries. An Indian woman named Short and Dirty shared his home. In 1962, a niece who had read an earlier account of Cunningham's life by the author, reacted positively. "I was charmed to learn of 'Short and Dirty' — whom Uncle Stephen naturally never mentioned to us. In a family largely composed of rather painfully respectable citizens, she is a delightful contrast."

Inevitably, anecdotes were told about Cunningham. Jack Leidig elaborated on the time a woman visitor, who had talked to the Guardian in the Grove, arrived at the Wawona Hotel and saw him lounging on the porch. "Why, Mr. Cunningham," she exclaimed in astonishment, "how did you get here so fast?"

"Why," he responded gravely, "I came on my ass, mam, on my ass." His faithful donkey had carried him down the short, steep "Lightning Trail."

Then there was the time he was returning from Mariposa with a wagon-load of groceries, including bacon, cheese, crackers, and a five gallon jug of whiskey, and hit a chuckhole, whereupon the demijohn broke. "There goes half my winter provisions," mourned Cunningham.

Winters were increasingly hard on the aging man, who suffered from bouts of la grippe. Although he owned 160 acres along the river, which he had home-steaded in 1887, he had no savings. However, he was a U.S. Army veteran and thus entitled to government care. In October, 1898, the old mountaineer signed himself into Sawtelle Veterans' Hospital in Southern California where he died ten months later.

Two families of rugged individuals, the Bruces and Gordons, were important in the development of the

Pike's voice, dress, exploits and tall tales made him a legend in his lifetime. (YNP Collection.)

47

Wawona Hotel, its support facilities, and the area. Beginning in 1878, Jean Washburn's versatile brother, Al Bruce, ran the Washburn sawmill, and his wife Azelia Van Campen Bruce worked in the hotel. Their loyalty to the Washburn and Cook families was reflected in the names of their children, Albert Henry, Jay Cook, and Henrietta. In fact, Henrietta's birth on March 13, 1884, took place in Jean and Henry Washburn's San Francisco home. Family solidarity cracked a few weeks after her arrival, because Bruce filed a claim to 160 acres in Section 35 on the north side of the Merced. Although that land was several miles by road from the Wawona Hotel, it included two scenic attractions, a ferny grotto and Chilnualna Falls where stages deposited tourists to "oh," "ah," and explore. A foot bridge, tables, benches, and a trail had been built under the Washburns' direction, and John had taken out a land claim but let it lapse. Bruce's move upset the brothers who were wary that he might engage in a competitive business.

According to Jay C. Bruce's autobiography, *Cougar Killer,* the Washburns fired Bruce and refused to sell him lumber. Family records show that baby Henrietta's name was promptly changed to Harriet! Within a couple of years, however, Bruce was hired as the hotel's blacksmith, Azelia was paid to sew pillow slips, linen sheets and napkins in their homestead house, and when another daughter was born in July, 1886, she was named Jean for her aunt. Later a son was called Edward Washburn Bruce, testifying that relationships remained good.

Even as youngsters, Bert and Jay were adept at supplying fish and game for the family, and, as teenagers, became part of the Washburn enterprises. Genial epicure Thomas Hill gave Jay a .22-caliber rifle and 500 BB caps with instructions to keep him supplied with quail, a task that launched Jay on his career as professional hunter.

In 1896, at 15, Jay went to work at the hotel. "The first few jobs were typical of the period," he wrote, "pick and shovel laborer on the road gang, farm hand, fire fighter, stage driver . . . The jobs were temporary — geared to the work that had to be done and to the season of the year." In 1899 he was milking cows, which he loathed, when the Indian who caught fish for the hotel quit and Jay was hired as replacement. Ah, heaven! "During the next two seasons of six months each, I whipped the trout streams four to eight hours per day and caught some 32,000 trout . . . It wasn't scarcity of fish that stopped me from continuing to supply the Wawona Hotel with trout, it was a law prohibiting the commercial sale of trout . . ."

From the 1860's the Gordon family was part of Wawona. As mentioned earlier, Peter Gordon, the redoutable Pete, was a pioneer guide. His son, Tom, went to work for "Uncle Henry" Washburn as a lad, and stayed until he was 69. Tom wasn't much over five feet tall, but sinewy and tough enough to handle the

Azelia V. Bruce had ten children (three died in infancy), and the drive to work at a variety of jobs including sewing 600 pieces of linen in one year for the Wawona Hotel. (Mary and A. W. Hood Collection.)

most spirited team in his years of driving stage. "Fastest trip I ever made," Tom remembered, "was from Miami to Ahwahnee, a distance of ten miles, in exactly 55 minutes. It must have been right, too, because Harriman, the railroad king, was along and timed us! I had no idea we were going so fast."

Tom Gordon's family consisted of six boys and three girls, three of whom are alive today. His sons, Tom, Jr., Joley, Henry, and Eddie all worked as stagedrivers. Ultimately three generations of Gordons lived in a house the Washburns built uphill from the hotel. Eddie was born in the same year Clarence Washburn was, 1886, and the two were lifelong friends. At 16, short but stalwart Eddie went to work at Wawona as a stockman; three years later he was driving stages into Yosemite Valley and did not retire from the Company until he was 82! Like his Dad, Eddie set some records. With eleven passengers holding tight, he inspired his team to negotiate the eight miles from Wawona Point, elevation 6,810 feet, to the hotel, at 4,000 feet, in 40 minutes. Eddie's career, as well as that of his wife, May, and children, Albert, Richard, and Gladys, is briefed later in this book. Today, 1979, as yesterday, 1879, and earlier, there are Bruces and Gordons in Wawona.

CHAPTER VIII

Henry Washburn

•

Even the springtime roar of the South Fork was diminished by the cadence of hoof beats on May 19, 1891, when two troops of cavalrymen trotted across the meadow. Their leader, a ramrod-straight officer, halted in front of the main Hotel where a crowd had gathered on the porch. "Captain A.E. Wood, commander of the Fourth Cavalry and acting superintendent of Yosemite National park, at your service," he announced. Wood, a Civil War veteran, West Point graduate, and Indian fighter, radiated authority.

"My orders are to set up camp at Wawona," the Captain said, then added, his face reddening, "If you could supply a guide to the site, I would appreciate it."

"Of course," Henry Washburn was hard-put not to smile. Glancing around, he spotted William M. Sell, Jr., astride his pinto pony. "Will, lead these gentlemen to their camp, please."

Moments later, eight-year-old Willie, shoulders square and face beaming with pride, trotted up the dusty road, followed by the U.S. Army.

Camp A.E. wood was promptly set up on a flat between the river and the Wawona Road, a mile north of the hotel. After that, Wood ordered patrols to explore the new national park, build trails, and make maps, jobs that were to take years of seasonal effort. The officers participated in naming many significant features, often for fellow officers. One exception was Washburn Lake, named for A.H. Washburn in 1895. By 1896, a "combat" role was added to the Army's

responsibilities; patrols ran sheep, cattle, and their infuriated owners, out of the Park.

On October 1, 1890, after a massive publicity campaign, spearheaded by John Muir and magazine editor, Robert Underwood Johnson, Congress had created Yosemite National Park, an enormous area of superb high country, surrounding the Yosemite Grant. Both the Mariposa Grove of Big Trees and Yosemite Valley continued to be administered by the State of California and its small band of civilian employees, while the Army was the protector of the Park.

Although the Wawona Basin was not included in either the Grant or the Park, it was affected by the military jurisdiction. "The Army made things more lively," recalled Charlotte Bruce, "as the wives and visitors came on the scene, and there was hardly an officer of any repute who did not make the trip to Yosemite or was stationed there . . ."

Soldiers lent flavor, charm, and romance to the scene. A uniformed officer added glamor to the hotel dining room, the dances, horseback rides, and strolls along the Brook Walk. Naturally, the three teenage Bruce girls gained admirers; in fact, two of them married officers later.

Washburn's daughter, Jeannie, had already married Charles Clum Higgins in March, 1889, when he was 26 and she 21. Presumably, they met through her uncle, J.J. Cook, for Higgins worked as a clerk in Cook's drug store in San Francisco. The couple's first child,

For years Roscoe Greeley's team of oxen were a familiar sight in the Wawona Basin. Logging and local mills supplied most of the lumber required in hotel buildings, (SS Collection.)

a son, died at birth, but a daughter was born later, and Grampa Henry had to be satisfied with Henrietta for a namesake. Later, C.C. Higgins, Jr., completed the family.

Charlie, Sr., was a Joe College-type who spouted slang, often stayed at the Wawona Hotel, worked there, and once engaged in an elaborate bear hunt. A pioneering cartoon strip of it appeared in a *San Francisco Call.* One picture showed the big-game hunter riding a bicycle toward a platform high up a pine, oblivious of birds on his gun barrel, and squirrels cavorting in front of him. The last picture showed Higgins determinedly mounting the ladder, while a bear jumped on his parked bike. The accompanying verse ran:

> Lord Higgins when he turned around
>   Saw the bear scorch o'er the ground.
> "How did he ride?" a friend asked that night.
>   Higgins said, "Out of sight."

Children were always a delight to Henry Washburn. ". . . at dinner time," his niece Charlotte recorded, "you could always see the children of those who worked for him standing around with pitchers and bowls ready to take home the ice cream they knew would be forthcoming." Just as regularly, the children of Mariposa campers showed up outside the kitchen where Ah You would bestow cookies and pieces of his famous apple pie upon them. To escape the heat, and open sewers, in Mariposa, a large number of families, e.g. the Schlageters, Ridgways, Linds, McElligots, Farnsworths, and others set up named camps near the covered bridge and spent summers there. The men either worked for the Washburns or came up for

weekends. Henry was loyal to Mariposa, where he had begun business, and employed many Mariposans.

In 1891 when Clarence Washburn reached school age, his father and uncles built a school for him and the local children. That same year the U.S. Fish Commission began shipping eastern brook trout to Captain Wood for stocking of lakes and streams. As fish were integral to the hotel menu, and to make fishermen-guests happy, Washburn built a fish hatchery in 1895, which was operated by the California Fish and Game Commission.

Henry inspired most of the homesteading on the south side of the Merced River, and later bought the acreage from the "homesteader" who, in reality, was either an employee, associate, or relative. For example, James Ridgway, stage driver and road foreman, homesteaded 160 acres, for which he received a patent, but sold it to Washburn in 1889 for "Consideration, $1.00." By 1891 A.H. owned 1,124 acres, and in partnership with J.J. Cook, another 661 acres. Brother John had a paltry 160 acres, and brother Ed kept his hands in his pockets.

On January 17, 1891, all land was granted to the Wawona Hotel Company, a new corporation formed by the three brothers, Cook, and his son. One hundred thousand shares of stock at $5.00 per share were subscribed. Henry bought 50,000, John and Ed 12,500 each, while Cook purchased 24,900 shares, and his son took the remaining 100. From that time on, the hotel, farming, trading, and commercial business was run by the Wawona Hotel Company and its directors, but, of course, A.H. Washburn was the boss.

His power was felt even in the politics revolving around successive governors who named Guardians for the Yosemite Grant. Inept ones followed Galen Clark's term, which had ended in 1880, so he was reappointed in 1889, at the age of 75, to serve for another seven years. His successors were politicians whose abilities did not fit their responsibilities.

"What Henry wanted, Henry got," Larry Degnan, knowledgable son of a Yosemite Valley pioneer, told the author. "Before the turn of the century he was gradually acquiring control of the big concessions in the Valley itself. This I know to be a fact: there was no pretense that the nominal holders of those concessions owed allegiance to, or took orders from, anybody but Henry Washburn. When James McCauley was hornswoggled out of his Glacier Point Hotel, who do you suppose was the successful bidder for the lease? John Stevens, one of Washburn's stage drivers."

"Nevertheless, Washburn was a good friend to our family," Degnan continued, "and when my oldest sister, Daisy, set out to study bookkeeping, telegraphy and the like, she lived at Washburn's home on Fillmore Street . . . Later, she had charge of the telegraph office and Wells Fargo at Wawona, although she was only in her teens . . ."

Washburn desired political help in the California

Washburn Lake was named for Henry Washburn in 1895 by an admiring Army officer. (Hank Johnston photograph.)

Legislature, so supported the election of Ed Baxter, grandson of Fannie and J.J. Cook. Baxter still spent much of his time at the Wawona Hotel or at the Washburn home in San Francisco. After his term as assemblyman, Baxter took Cunningham's place as guide and curio seller at the Mariposa Grove. Baxter, Bruce Leitch, and a large number of shirttail relatives were, in the words of contemporaries, "freeloaders." The Washburn family table in the hotel dining room seated eight, but often a second table was needed for friends and relatives. Not only were their meals complimentary, but Washburn supplied them with rooms, transportation, and even riding horses.

Whenever a Bruce or Sell family member traveled to San Francisco, they stayed with the Washburns at the Palace Hotel, or at 2525 Fillmore for long periods, and "never thought a thing about it." Mrs. Washburn had become a semi-invalid and stayed upstairs, propped by pillows, expectant of attention.

Washburn spent little time at his hotel-like City home, for he and his brothers rarely left Wawona until early January, and returned in March to ready things for opening about April 1. When he was in San Francisco, he was wheeling and dealing with Southern Pacific officials, travel agencies and publicity people. So allied was he with the Southern Pacific Railroad that he had an office in their building. The S.P.'s monopoly of the San Joaquin Valley had ended in 1896 when a rival company, later called the Santa Fe, built a railroad through it. Washburn never relaxed efforts to have rails extended to his forested domain, and backed several abortive plans, including an electric railway from Raymond to Wawona.

Superintendent, Yosemite Stage & Turnpike Co. was Henry Washburn's favorite title, and he took pride in his position and company, which he operated with efficiency. It was a large enterprise with a peak of 600-700 horses, and 25 stages, plus numerous freight wagons, water carts, buggies, and other conveyances. Each stage was resplendently red, with a yellow undercarriage and black and gold lettering on the sides. They began each run clean and shiny, ended brown with dust. Horses were husky, handsome, and matched for looks, strength, and compatibility. Planning the matched teams was one of Washburn's winter jobs, and later, of his chief assistant, Sam Owens. Both men loved horses and would not allow them to be mistreated. As mentioned earlier, stables were maintained at all 10 or 12 stage stops, plus Raymond and Yosemite Valley.

In 1893, Washburn purchased a large acreage near Madera for a winter headquarters. Sam Owens was

Invariably enterprising and innovative, Washburn, holding reins, had a stage placed atop the Fallen Monarch. Thomas Hill appears at right on the front seat and Estella Hill Washburn is standing behind him. (George Fiske photograph; WWH Collection.)

named foreman of the Stage Ranch, and saw to the development of fencing, growing hay and grain, a pumping plant, and three large barns. One was for storage, painting, and repair of vehicles; one for the horses; and the third for the dairy cows that were driven there after the hotel closed. Herding them back and forth was a tedious trip requiring about seven days each way. Sam's son John went to work herding cows at age ten.

In 1885, 2,590 people visited Yosemite, in 1899, 4,500, and in 1902, 8,023! Henry Washburn hired more drivers, bought more horses, and ordered more stages, but more hotel rooms were also needed. By the spring of 1895, an "elegant," two-storied cottage, topped by a roomy cupola, stood on the hill directly back of the Main Hotel. It was ornamented by Vic-

torian fretwork, encircled by a wide, roofed porch, and contained five high-ceilinged rooms on the first floor, and five small odd-shaped, low-ceilinged bedrooms on the second.

Along about then, more dormer windows were added in the attic of the Long White to light 12 bedrooms. No baths existed on either floor, although toilets and lavatories were in a lean-to at the south end of the building. Bathtubs were available only upstairs in the main hotel.

Despite the new rooms, tents had to be set up to house employees. Late in 1899, carpenters began a new 42 x 96-foot porch-encircled one-story building with eleven bedrooms. After it was painted brown, it was called the Long Brown. Similarly, the cupolaed cottage became the Little Brown.

In 1893-94 a cupolaed guest cottage, named the Little Brown for its size and color, was added to the Wawona Hotel complex. Fountain and weathervane no longer exist, but the intricate scroll-work, and the now-towering Sequoia trees do. (Herbert W. Gleason photograph, 1909; Roland Wells Robbins Gleason Collection.)

Throughout the years of separation, the Washburns of Wawona had urged brother Julius to visit them. He had stayed on the family farm in Putney, raising tobacco, and caring for their mother until her death. He had seven children, one of whom died, by three wives, two of whom died. When he needed money, Edward responded. Finally in July, 1898, Sarah Washburn, the oldest of the children, came west. Uncle Ed arranged railroad passes for her and suggested she might teach school. "But as we run both hotels in Yosemite (Valley), we might give her a position, if desired, in the business," he wrote Julius and his wife Mary, reflecting the Washburn-Cook dominance of the Valley's concessions. "We have to have in both places a Post Office, Telegraph Office and an Express Office that desire considerable attention . . ."

In October, Julius, Mary, and their three youngest children, Abby, Harold Edward, and William, joined Sarah and the Californians for a grand reunion. Their long stay at Wawona, and in San Francisco, had a lasting effect in which Henry's powerful hand can be discerned. Afterwards, Julius sold tobacco to Miller and Lux, maple syrup to the hotel, and recommended Vermonters for jobs at Wawona. Indeed, Mary's brother worked for the Company, and Julius strongly considered selling his farm, moving to Wawona, and investing in the Company. That never materialized, but, as his health was poor, he spent most winters with his brothers.

On June 24, 1900, history arrived at the Wawona Hotel in a two cylinder, ten horsepower, gasoline-powered Locomobile. Not only was the 640-pound vehicle a curious sight, but its corpulent, 300-pound driver-owner, Oliver Lippincott, a conversation piece. His bulk left only a niche for a mechanic on the narrow seat. Despite their combined weight, and that of extra gasoline, the Locomobile had traversed the 44 miles and steep grades between Raymond and Wawona in five hours and eighteen minutes, roughly half the time it took a stage.

Henry was so entranced by the machine that he accompanied it to Yosemite Valley, then persuaded Lippincott to drive to Glacier Point. That was accomplished in five hours, part of the way in darkness. Tom Gordon followed with a team and wagon that were needed to help a couple of times. "Nothing would do the next morning but that the locomobile must go out on the overhanging rock where only the most fearless and level-headed have ever dared to stand," wrote Lippincott. Burnett, a Stanford athlete, and Washburn tied ropes around their waists, then pulled the Locomobile out on the jutting suspension while other men pushed and women "buried their heads in their hands, horrified at the sight . . ."

"At last," Lippincott continued, "it was out in a firm position, and we grouped ourselves around it, fairly hanging on with tooth and nail, while the camera was adjusted. No picture was ever so long in being taken.

I was sure I felt the rock shaking under me."

Intrepid, innovative transportation-king Washburn was convinced that automobiles were the answer to fast, efficient transport. He corresponded with a manufacturer in New York, and in November, 1901, had an "eight-passenger auto" tested on the road between Raymond and Wawona. After that, he traveled to New York himself to discuss motorized stages.

Until adequate vehicles materialized, or he could influence a railroad being built into the mountains, Washburn's chief concern was to maintain the best possible service on his stage line. In June, 1901, the Yosemite Stage & Turnpike Co. introduced the Cannonball Stage, which traversed the 72 rugged miles from Raymond to Yosemite Valley in 12 hours. Teams were changed every seven or eight miles, and traveled at a trot uphill and down. Each morning one stage left from Raymond, another from the Valley. A quick lunch stop was made at the Wawona Hotel. Despite its bone-jolting attributes, the Cannonball was so popular seats were booked months in advance. In addition, the traditional, regular schedule of stage travel was maintained.

In June of the following year, the stage company experimented with oiling the Raymond-Wawona Road, another first in the Sierra. Dust was a great annoyance that not even water wagons, which were in use, could effectively subdue. J.J. Cook owned some oil wells near Santa Barbara and had impressed Washburn with the efficacy of the black gold. Large storage tanks were erected at the Company ranch near Madera, and sprinkling wagons applied oil several times that summer. Cost was in excess of $10,000, but the effect

While "women buried their heads in their hands," with horror Washburn engineered the first automobile to visit Yosemite out upon a precarious perch on the Overhanging Rock at Glacier Point. (Los Angeles County Museum of Natural History Collection.)

was laudable.

That Henry Washburn was not indestructible was first realized by the family in the winter of 1898-99 when at 64 he was seriously ill. Other illnesses followed but nothing kept him from his beloved Wawona Hotel. In 1902, he returned to San Francisco before October 1, for on that date he signed a simple two-page will leaving $1,500 each to his wife, Fannie, Alice, and Charlotte Bruce. All the rest of his considerable estate was given to his brothers "to hold, manage and control, invest and reinvest" so that one-half of the income would go to his wife and the other half to his daughter in monthly installments.

Twenty-four days later, Albert Henry Washburn was dead. His illness, newspapers reported, was brief; acute gastritis had sent him to a hospital where he died of a "hemmorage of the brain" at 2 p.m. October 25. His funeral in St. Paul's Episcopal Church was well-attended by friends and civic figures. Honorary pall-bearers included his lawyer and a Yosemite Valley Commissioner, while active pallbearers were composed of stage drivers Tom Gordon, Sam Owens, Henry Hedges, Sam Uren, "Stonewall Jackson" Ashworth, E.J. White, Jim Warner, and C.K. Salmon.

Henry Washburn's death created a tremendous void in Yosemite; gone was the leadership and vision that had developed roads, transportation, and the services of the Wawona Hotel; gone was the genial spirit, the soft touch and support, moral and financial, which had been bestowed on a multitude of people. "Of the hundred or more men whom he employed," Charlotte Bruce said, "there was not one who wouldn't have risked his life for him."

Among the tributes was an unpublished but eloquent one written by Alice Bruce to bereft "Uncle Ed." "No one will ever know how much I loved your brother. All the love that would have gone to father and mother went to him."

CHAPTER IX

Uncle Ed and the 20th Century

•

Within three years of Washburn's death, the transportation and political domination, so long enjoyed by the brothers and their Yosemite Stage & Turnpike Co., were ended by the very item they had sought for years — a railroad. But the rails, laid between 1905 and 1907, were far from Wawona. Instead they were spiked down from Merced, up the north side of the hitherto inaccessible Merced River Canyon, to a point 10 miles west of Yosemite Valley itself. At that wide space in the canyon, a railway terminus, station, and town were built. It was named El Portal, the gateway, and within months after daily trains began operating on May 15, 1907, superseded the old gateway, Raymond. In fact, the Southern Pacific ceased operations to Raymond in 1910. The S.P.'s loss was minimal, however, as most Yosemite-bound train passengers rode S.P. trains to Merced where they transferred to the Yosemite Valley Railroad. It was financed and built by a group of Bay Area businessmen without prior railway experience.

Trains were met at the El Portal station by stages belonging to the Yosemite Transportation Company, a rival outfit, for the last few miles of travel over a new, riverside road into Yosemite Valley. Had not the Mariposa Grove existed so close to Wawona, the Wawona Hotel and its complex of satellite enterprises might have gone bankrupt. But the Sequoias continued to be a tourist magnet, and travelers stayed at Wawona and used the Yosemite Stage & Turnpike stages.

Nevertheless, there was a sharp decrease in patronage.

Henry's leadership, vision, and combativeness were sorely missed. Although John and Edward Washburn were excellent hotel men, neither had the experience or personality to anticipate or out-maneuver the transportation competition. Eventually, the brothers made a deal with the Yosemite Valley Railroad Company so they could operate stages from El Portal to Yosemite Valley and on to Wawona and the Mariposa Grove.

Automobiles, Henry had said, were the key to future business, but autos were not allowed inside Yosemite National Park because the Secretary of the Interior ruled the condition of Yosemite roads unfit for the combined operation of teams and automobiles. Thus it was that autoists could drive only as far as Wawona, then had to park, and climb aboard a horse-powered stage for the trip to Yosemite Valley. Still some people realized that what the railroad had done to stages, autos would do to the railroad. In anticipation of that, the Washburns supported Edwin T. Huffman, from the Crocker-Huffman ranch near Merced, when he organized the Madera, Yosemite, Big Trees Auto Company in 1913.

Age took toll of the principals of the Wawona Hotel Company. Both Jean Bruce Washburn and J.J. Cook died in 1904, and long-ailing Thomas Hill in 1908. Management was troubled anew when Jeannie and Charles Higgins contested John and Ed's executorship of Henry's will. Jeannie Higgins had replaced her father as a director of the Company, and she and her husband had large ideas of expanding it as a Del Monte-type resort. Higgins wanted management changes, "purely business proposition," he wrote, "irrespective of anyone's feelings." By April, 1904, a letter indicates that new help, and sweeping changes were in effect —" . . . new book-keeper and a brand new set of books . . . more red tape than the U.S. gov. . . . when Edward wants a nickel to pay for a shine he has to ask for it." Meticulous, bookkeeping Ed had been deposed, and the Higgins faction appeared dominant.

However, a strong ally, business head, and leader was developing for the aging brothers in the lean, athletic figure of Clarence A. Washburn. From childhood, he had known every facet of hotel life, and had done everything from making beds and emptying chamberpots to registering guests and arranging stage seating. His favorite work was fishing. His record catch was 297 in a single day. One fall, when he went off to the University of California, he had $400 earned from catching fish.

Graduation from Cal in 1907, where his major was civil engineering, completed an education begun in Wawona's one-room school in 1891. At the age of 21, he married, and went to work as a hotel clerk. In 1908 he became assistant manager, in charge of transportation.

Early that same year, a power plant providing 500 lights was installed. By June 20, it was "working in perfect order . . ." the *Gazette* reported. Maintaining "perfect order" involved an electrician, a ditch keeper, and the Washburns, as the water flow had to be at a certain level to keep the buildings lit. A system of headgates with removable boards, floats, and signal lights evolved. Within a few years, a Pelton wheel and a small gasoline engine to help out in the peak hours of use were added. Every morning one of the Washburns or Eddie Gordon took the Brook Walk to check the ditch for obstructions or cave-ins. Although refrigeration was a boon in the hotel kitchens, ice cut on Stella Lake was still used. After 11 p.m., only some dim porch lights burned except in the dance hall near the store where dances were even more enjoyable under illumination.

Precise Ed had mellowed with age, but his sense of humor had sharpened. Before the turn of the century, a guest had remarked that he had traveled over the world and patronized the finest hotels and restaurants, and now at Wawona found one item that was unexcelled anywhere else. Flattered, Ed asked, "Pray, what is that?" "The salt," replied the practical joker. "Oh, pshaw," Ed exclaimed disgustedly.

By 1909 he displayed wit in writing Alice Bruce that he was going to spend part of the winter at San Francisco's new, after-the-earthquake Palace Hotel. "Should we conclude that the style there is up to our requirements. Would not like to patronize a Hotel

that will detract from our standards in the social world."

For decades Uncle Ed had been a soft touch for the three Bruce girls, Jeannie Washburn, and Clarence. After Henry's death, he was more of a father to the Bruces, even giving Charlotte away at her marriage. In 1901, Fannie wed Lieutenant Joseph I. McMullen, ending her brief career as the hotel's telegraph operator. Charlotte attended Stanford, then taught the Wawona School in the July-till-snow 1903-05 sessions. On Thanksgiving Day, 1905, Ed Washburn turned her over to Lieutenant Herbert Charles Gibner, an Army doctor, in a colorful wedding ceremony at the hotel. Pine boughs, Woodwardia ferns, and the pennants of Yale and Stanford, the couple's alma maters, decorated the parlor. Soon afterward, the Gibners left for the Philipines, in the first of many Army moves. Yet Charlotte never forgot Wawona as evidenced by nostalgic memoirs written in 1955 and quoted in this history.

Only Alice Bruce remained unaffected by the Army, but had a Yosemite romance. She married John Garibaldi, a storekeeper in the Valley, and later Merced.

Two young mountaineers, Will Sell Jr. and Clarence Washburn, attended the University of California at Berkeley after the turn of the century. J.J. Cook's associate, photographer I.W. Taber, took their pictures as he had of other Washburn family members. (WWH Collection.)

Ed Washburn is seated next to the driver on the front seat
while his nephew watches from the porch. Estella Washburn
is shown shaking hands with a passenger. (YPC&C Co.
Collection.)

Willeta Hill and Estella Washburn
bidding President Theodore Roosevelt
goodbye after he visited Thomas
Hill's Studio in May, 1903. (YNP Collection.)

There was a rash of stage hold-ups in 1905-06 but most passengers found them exciting. One woman, from whom $20 was taken, said, "I wouldn't have missed it for one hundred!" In August, 1905 a fearless hold-up man posed obligingly for this picture. (WWH Collection.)

She had a fine collection of Indian baskets, and was esteemed by her contemporaries and her Uncle Ed to whom she gave a daughterly love and concern.

Thanksgiving was a big day at the hotel, but Christmas was even more gala. "We had the usual Christmas turkey," Ed Washburn wrote Alice about the 1909 observance, "the beautiful Christmas tree larger and more beautiful than ever before, and the table was covered with Christmas presents more numerous than ever." Christmas carols, with Estella Washburn leading the singers, was another traditional pleasure.

After Julius' visit in 1898, he returned virtually every winter to visit at Wawona and at the Washburns' winter quarters — a suite at the Palace. Ironically, he was the only Washburn to die at Wawona. On August 11, 1907, aged 67, Julius dropped dead from a heart attack while back of the main building. Ed continued to help Julius' wife and children. He paid for Abby's tuition at telegraphy school, then employed her at Wawona, and helped the two boys through Dartmouth.

When Ed made his will on February 6, 1909, he left one-half of his estate to his brother, John, and the other half to John and Clarence in trust for the children of Julius, to be paid annually from "rents, profits, and income thereof . . ." So did kindly, generous Ed continue to provide for the four nieces and two nephews. Eventually, one nephew, Harold Edward Washburn, married and had two sons, John, presently a lawyer and Soviet Affairs Specialist, and Wilcomb, a historian at the Smithsonian Institution. William Washburn, Julius' second son, became a noted surgeon in San Francisco. He fathered a daughter, and three sons, one, fittingly named, Edward.

Within two years of making his will, Edward Payson Washburn, 76, died, not in the Wawona Hotel, but in a simple, style-less cottage belonging to the Wawona Hotel Company in Raymond, on December 14, 1911. Services were held in San Francisco's Grace Cathedral, and burial was at Cypress Lawn.

Edward's estate, consisting of 2,500 shares of stock in the Wawona Hotel Company, 2,756¼ shares in the Yosemite Stage & Turnpike Co., and several savings accounts, was appraised at over $72,000, but his personal possessions were meager. He owned a Thomas Hill painting of Upper Chilnualna Falls, valued at $40, half interest in two others, a stem-winding gold watch and chain, gold cuff buttons, and a small diamond shirt stud.

Before his death, Ed had participated in arrangements for the visits of U.S. Presidents Theodore Roosevelt and William Howard Taft at the Wawona Hotel. In mid-May, 1903, Roosevelt was there but scorned a bed at the hotel in favor of sleeping on the ground beside John Muir under the Sequoias in the Mariposa Grove. However, he stopped at the hotel and charmed everyone he met. While touring Thomas Hill's Studio, he admired a large painting of Bridalveil Fall, which the artist immediately gave him. Alice Bruce loaned him her horse to ride on the three-day trip with Muir. Before he, Muir, and two packers were left in the Grove, the Washburns hosted the president with a champagne lunch there.

Later Roosevelt left the Park on the "Cannonball Stage," which stopped for lunch at Wawona. He was so impressed with the delicious pie that he sought out Ah You to compliment him. Additionally, he told Alice Bruce that her "magnificent horse" had been "the means of giving me three of the most delightful days in my life."

On October 7, 1909, the Little White was a temporary "White House," as President Taft spent a night in it. John Muir was with him, and U.S. Army Cavalrymen guarded him. On the following day, Muir guided Taft through the Mariposa Grove. Presumably, John Washburn, whose first wife had been related to the President, enjoyed a visit with Taft.

Certainly those visitations had given the Wawona Hotel the "standing in the social world" Ed Washburn had teased Alice about. For both, he had probably worn his best bib and tucker, gold cuff buttons, and diamond shirt stud.

CHAPTER X

The Auto Age

•

When the Wawona Hotel opened in April, 1912, a father and son management team welcomed guests. Courtly John Washburn, 73, was the manager, and Clarence, 25, had been appointed as second-in-command. Besides youthful vigor and ideas, Clarence possessed a lot of his father's diplomacy and some of his Uncle Henry's competitiveness. He was planning ahead to the long anticipated time when automobiles would be allowed to travel in Yosemite. When that red-letter day arrived on August 22, 1913, however, traffic was admitted only on the Coulterville Road. It was August 8, 1914, before cars were finally allowed to travel from Wawona to Yosemite Valley. Horse and auto stages shared the road until April, 1916, when the Washburns retired the horses.

June 17, 1914, was also noteworthy. On that date a birth took place in the hotel. Clarence Washburn's first marriage had resulted in divorce; his second in 1913, was to Grace Brinkop whose son, Thomas, he adopted later. Medical assistance was planned for the advent of their baby, but the infant arrived a week early. As the first cries were heard, guests on the porch below exclaimed, "There's little Wawona!" Although her parents named her Estella Florence to commemorate her grandmothers, so many people called her Wawona that the name adhered, then and now. After her father's death in 1972, Wawona checked his diary to see what he had written about her momentous birth and was chagrined to find only the laconic comment, "Baby born." (That entry was typical of the daily journal kept by Clarence Washburn: terse, simple statements, but valuable today as documentation.)

During 1914, civilian rangers, who became part of the National Park Service when it was created two years later, replaced the Army in managing and protecting Yosemite National Park. One of them, Alan Sproul, 18, was stationed at the Mariposa Grove, but spent leisure time at the hotel, which in retrospective remarks, he pictured as a sleepy place. "The guests, if they stayed more than overnight, were supposed to be happy just to be there and do nothing. There was no swimming pool, the meadow was still a hayfield and pasture . . . The scenery and the climate provided the pleasures of the spirit and a Chinese cook provided good food . . . The porch was full of rocking chairs, and a dreamy, dusty calm surrounded the enchanted spot . . .

"Old John Washburn . . . with his full white beard and general elder-of-the-church appearance . . . provided the place with an air of pioneer dignity . . . The whole was run by his son, Clarence, who was responsible for the hotel's tennis court, but who otherwise hadn't changed things much. Finally, there was an itinerant barber, a godsend to travelers and rangers. The rigors of a life as a ranger at Camp A.E. Wood or Mariposa Grove in 1914 were certainly tempered by the amenities of the Wawona Hotel."

On August 8, 1914 the first private car, a Studebaker belonging to Chester N. Weaver, a frequent Wawona Hotel guest, was allowed to drive from the hotel into Yosemite Valley. On June 2, 1915, the Washburns instituted daily auto stages. Clarence Washburn is standing at right of the first car. (WWH Collection.)

Baby Wawona with Grandfather John Washburn and a snowy friend. (WWH Collection.)

With the advent of automobiles, guests demanded a greater variety of entertainment. Their wishes enabled Clarence to persuade his father, mother, and the Higgins family, as directors of the Wawona Hotel Company, to finance extensive improvements. It may be assumed that Charlie Higgins backed him. His wife and children still spent summers at the hotel. Board meetings were held at the Company's office in San Francisco, and plans made for an extensive expansion program. Hill's former studio was remodeled into a Club House with a dance floor and soda fountain, a croquet court was installed, and plans made for a swimming "tank," and golf course. A second floor, with ten guestrooms and four baths, was added to the Long Brown, and a large dining room and new kitchen to the Main Hotel. The old dining are evolved into a lounge. Even Stella Lake was upgraded with a boathouse and new rowboat.

John Washburn's long tenure at Wawona ended on June 14, 1917, although he died in an Oakland hospital rather than at the place he had loved so well. His beautiful and gentle wife, who lived until 1950, and Clarence were with him. Improvements at the hotel continued because the directors of the Wawona Hotel Company promptly appointed Clarence as General Manager. That summer the swimming "tank" was finished, and fishing and camping trips into the high country introduced. Pierce-Arrow autos could be rented at $4.00 an hour for tours around the meadow, to Signal Park, or the Mariposa Grove. Most exciting of all, Clarence supervised the laying out of the first mountain golf course in the state.

As soon as the hotel closed in the fall of 1917, carpenters and plasterers moved into the main building to remodel the former Washburn rooms, parlor, and the office. Mrs. John moved into a room upstairs, although her piano remained on the first floor, a gathering place for guests whenever she played. Clarence and his family lived high above the new dining room in an attic. Its charm was diminished by summer heat. Before snowfall, construction began on a large, two-story building that was to contain 39 guest rooms, 21 baths, a roomy lounge with a cobblestone fireplace, and covered porches. From the beginning, it was known as the Annex. Plumbing and electrical shops were set up in the basement, which also provided quarters for a golf shop and shower rooms.

As soon as the snow melted the following spring, a new sewer ditch was dug in front of the hotel, lobby and dining rooms were finished, the Annex opened, and the golf course had its first players. On May 23 young Thomas Washburn ran up a flag on a new flagpole by the fountain as the school children sang the "Star Spangled Banner."

The August 10, 1918, issue of *Western Hotels and Travel* applauded the improvemetns at the Wawona Hotel, and its manager. "Mr. Washburn has shown remarkable ability and enterprise in carrying out the work of his father . . . His ideas are progressive and he typifies that rare quality that stands out from the rest in the born hotel man . . . He is a 'real fellow,' made up of qualities, force and friendliness that show up in his efforts to make Wawona second to none of the mountain resorts in California."

World War I had little effect on Wawona, though after the Armistice Yosemite travel jumped from 35,527 to 58,362 in 1919. During the roaring 20's, travel doubled, tripled, and skyrocketed to a total of over 461,000 in 1929. In 1919, 126 guest rooms had seemed adequate, but within a couple of years, there was TRO (tent room only). Tents rented at $4.50 a day, as did rooms without bath in the Main Hotel and Long White; charges were higher in the Long Brown, $5.00 for a single without bath and $6.00 with. Even the steam-heated, bathroom-equipped Annex rooms were reasonable, $7.00 for a single, $13.00 for a double.

Much of the revenue went into maintenance and additons. "Men layed foundation for new store building. Hole for cellar nearly finished." Clarence recorded on March 18, 1920. It was finished and open that year, as was a new men's bunkhouse, and a "girl's house." Simultaneously Clarence commented on the routine ranch operations: pasturing lambs in the meadow for 40c per lamb per month, getting extra woodchoppers, cutting the hay in the meadow, digging potatoes, pruning fruit trees (a two-week job), putting up new fences, fixing the floor of the ice house, and building a new slaughter house and

Dusty tourists posed beside the last word in Pierce-Arrow auto stages about 1920 the year the new store opened. Ed Huffman who managed the Madera Yosemite-Big Tree Auto Co. owned 35% of the stock while the Wawona Hotel Co. retained the rest . . . (SS Collection.)

In June of 1918, the new Annex, the swimming "tank," and the Wawona golf course opened so Wawona was "second to none of the mountain resorts in California." (Postcard from SS Collection.)

This still-flowing fountain was built in 1918 to replace an earlier one. (WWH Collection.)

A second floor and attached bathrooms were added to the Long Brown, now called Washburn Cottage, in 1905. This view is of the back. (YP & C. Co. Collection.)

The spacious new dining room, with adjoining kitchen, was a major addition. (YNP Collection.)

corrals. "Last beef will be killed in old one tomorrow," Clarence wrote. And a mid-December entry ran, "Turned electric lights off. Ditch too frozen to run them any longer."

To help with the outside operations of the hotel, Clarence turned to his boyhood friend and fishing companion, Eddie Gordon. A close bond persisted between the Gordon and the Washburn families.

In winter Clarence made monthly trips to Wawona over the old Chowchilla Mountain Road, by auto as far as possible, then by horse and wagon or sled. Often the family accompanied him to spend winter weeks at the hotel. They turned the old dining room into a "sitting room" with a wood stove for heat, but they had meals at the Gordon home up the hill. When snow melted off the roads, horses, cattle, hogs, sheep, and employees reactivated the grounds and buildings. Many cooks, waitresses, maids, and porters returned year after year; a head waitress presided over the dining room, and a housekeeper over that department. In the office, besides Clarence, there were two desk clerks at the busy time of the year, a bookkeeper, telephone operator, and a secretary. A hostess, who saw to the recreational needs of the guests, completed the staff.

Through the 20's, Charles Stephan was head electrician and in charge of the power plant. Three former stage drivers were employed, Tom Gordon in the boiler house, Jack Ashworth as night watchman, and Charlie Fobes as painter. No old-timer who wanted work was ever turned down by the Washburns. Traditionally, the cooks had been instructed not to let anyone go away hungry. One time Clarence asked a tramp who was eating in the kitchen, "can you chop wood?" A quarter of a century later, woodchopper Jack Davis estimated that he had cut enough wood to make a stack four feet high between Wawona and San Francisco.

Bald-headed, squinty-eyed Ah You was no longer chief baker, but peeled vegetables on the back porch, revered by the other Chinese cooks. As late as 1919, however, Ah You baked pies. When Park Service Director Steve Mather and Yosemite Superintendent W.B. Lewis had dinner at the hotel in May of that year, "They praised the meal and took two of Ah You's pies on to Yosemite with them." Ah You was succeeded by Ah Louie, and his apple pies and brown bread were also acclaimed.

". . . as we approached the hotel our nostrils were regaled with the celestial aroma of something baking," recalled Hil Oehlmann of a 1916 trip with three companions, including Don Tresidder. "Having lived on beans and cornmeal . . .the hiker's fare in those days, we automatically gravitated toward the kitchen. The cook, whom we engaged in friendly discourse, displayed keen interest in our travels. The incredible result was that we emerged with a freshly baked apple pie and a large loaf of bread that was still warm." In

On December 8, 1925, two Army pilots landed the first airplanes on the 3000 foot long Wawona field. Two years later Frank Gallison began daily flights, carrying passengers, mail, newspapers and a few light-weight supplies. (WWH Collection.)

years to come, Oehlmann and Tresidder were to have a far closer knowledge of the culinary department, and the hotel.

Although a U.S. Army airplane had caused a sensation by landing in Yosemite Valley in 1919, no pilot had dared attempt to set down in the Wawona meadow. As early as 1920, however, Clarence began a campaign for a landing field and eventually flagged a 3,000-foot strip. On December 8, 1925, a Lieutenant Moore landed at 12:40, followed by Lieutenant Taylor at 12:55, an hour and a half's flight from San Francisco. After that pilots dropped in occasionally. At first, upon hearing a plane, it was Wawona Washburn's job to jump on her horse, race up to the meadow landing area, and chase the stock into another pasture. Later, a fence was built to restrain the animals.

"I can testify to the thrill, as the quick trip over the mountains left me in doubt several times whether this trip was really necessary. And in the steep descent the landing strip looked smaller than a dime . . ." recorded Oehlmann, "but thanks to Frank Gallison's skill, we always got home safely."

Gallison, a native of Mariposa, was an expert pilot with experience in crop dusting and cross country flights. In 1927 with two other men he organized the Merced and Wawona Airline. "At a date no later than June 1" promised the *Mariposa Gazette*, "these enterprising young men hope to have their new

Yosemite photographer Arthur Pillsbury was a man after Henry Washburn's heart. With the aid of a ramp and a lot of brawny men, he lifted an auto stage atop the Fallen Monarch. (WWH Collection.)

machine, an Alexander Eagle Rock 90 horse-power biplane, in readiness for the initial flight between Merced and Wawona, following which a daily schedule will be followed with special sightseeing trips and taxi service over Yosemite and the High Sierras." Gallison flew in passengers, mail, San Francisco newspapers, and a few light-weight supplies. Airtime from Merced was 50 minutes, while flight from San Francisco took about two hours. Several Bay Area executives left their families at the hotel for a month or six weeks, but joined them for weekends by flying in with Gallison.

Everybody in the area, employees, guests, local residents, and visitors from surrounding counties, was invited for the fun, competitive events, and fireworks of the annual Fourth of July extravaganzas. There were foot and swimming races for the children, a golf tournament with elegant prizes, and always a rodeo and baseball game. As many as 3,000 people attended. The whole celebration was climaxed with a lively crowded dance. Clarence Washburn had been on the University of California baseball team, and took great pride in his Wawona Hotel team on which he played first base. Opposition was furnished by teams from Yosemite, Mariposa, and Sugar Pine.

From 1900 until 1931 the Madera Sugar Pine Company logged the crests south and west of Wawona. Sugar Pine, the headquarters of mill, store, and housing, even had a hospital with a doctor where Wawona residents could get treatment. The Wawona Hotel Company sold timber rights on some of its 2,665 acres to the logging company. Inevitably, loggers enlivened the Saturday night dances at the hotel, and their baseball team provided the Wawona team with its toughest competition. Baseball and golf were up-to-date activities for a resort, but apple pies, rocking chairs, and personal service remained a part of the traditional hospitality.

Chapter XI

The Last of the Washburns

During the 1920's several business enterprises constituted minor competition to the Wawona Hotel, but Clarence Washburn maintained rapport with their owners. Charles H. Murphy, a native of Vermont, had traded acreage near Signal Peak to the Madera Sugar Pine Company in exchange for P.R. Gipson's old ranch and orchard. One of the logging railroads crossed the property, and Murphy's daughter, Erma M. Fitzpatrick, recalled, "There were a number of logging camps surrounding our ranch. My father had a general store and did a thriving business with the loggers and their families. Our store supplied many of their needs — food, work clothes, shoes, dry goods, thread, needles, etc., and since prohibition had not yet gone into effect, wines, liquor and beer."

Additionally, the Murphys had a small rooming house, a gas pump, cows, a horse, and a produce garden. Twice-weekly in summer, Murphy delivered 80 to 100 baskets of strawberries to the Wawona Hotel, but sold his apple crop to a San Francisco wholesaler. Deer Glen was his name for the place.

As Murphy was a carpenter and in 1910 had married an Irish woman with two boys, he remodeled and enlarged Gipson's old cabin into a roomy, modern, shingled home. In time it was filled with five more Murphys. They attended the Wawona School, of which he was a trustee. Both parents died before 1928. Washburn bought Murphy's store stock, truck, cows, and other items in the estate, and staged a baseball game,

with Don Tresidder pitching, to benefit the orphaned children. Today, the picturesque ranch, still owned by Murphys, has been cleared of buildings, yet retains its rustic charm.

For a few years, Sierra Lodge, built in 1920, presented far more competition to the Wawona Hotel than did Murphy's. In the first place, it was only a half mile away from the hotel, and in the second place, its manager, Jack Minesini, was aggressively seeking tourist trade. His approach road took off above the east end of Stella Lake where a large archway, lighted at night, proclaimed SIERRA LODGE. That intrigued, and sometimes attracted hotel guests using the lake. Another advertising device, which infuriated Washburn, was a truck adorned with SIERRA LODGE signs and directional arrows, which Minesini left parked near the covered bridge, and on occasion drove slowly past the hotel buildings. Washburn's biggest conflict with Minesini was over the newcomer's unauthorized use of water. He had a shallow well dug near the Washburn Ditch, then inserted pipes between the two. Water, conflict, and confrontations ensued.

Louise and Jack Minesini had purchased 57 acres of meadow and logged slopes, built a steam-driven light plant, dining room-kitchen building, a dancehall, housekeep-ing cabins, a bath house, and a rooming house that resembled the Long White. Sierra Lodge enjoyed patronage because it was an up-to-date place, Italian meals with red wine were a novelty, and Mrs.

Minesini's piano playing popular. However, both of the Minesinis died in the '20s, so the business closed.

For a year or two, the property was operated by Sara Scroggs, who was principal of a private school in San Francisco, as a summer camp for children. Camp usage posed no threat to the Wawona Hotel, but when a section of the Ditch washed out and damaged the property, Washburn had to compensate Mrs. Scroggs. In the 1940's, the Park Service purchased the property and razed the structures.

In 1929, a Seventh Day Adventist summer camp was set up for children near Sierra Lodge. Clara Wolfsen, the first woman ranger in Yosemite, was the camp naturalist. In 1930, the Adventists bought three acres on a mountainside two miles up the river from the hotel, and began what is now a 30-acre complex with many substantial buildings, a swimming pool, rodeo grounds, and riding trails. In winter, the facilities are used for church conventions.

Across the river on land Hattie Bruce gave her father-in-law, James Spelt built four cabins of slab lumber cut in the Bruce sawmill. He called the place Camp Chilnualna and sold it to a Mrs. Wooster in 1926. In 1933, she rented the cabins to employees of the Granite Construction Company who were paving the new highway. Later one of them, Harold May, bought the camp. Today his son, Norman, continues to run it with modern cabins.

A number of other men who lived in or near Wawona while working on the new highway liked the area with its fishing and hunting so well that they stayed on. Most of them bought lots from the Bruce heirs, who in the 1920's and '30's subdivided and sold the 320 acres homesteaded by Azelia and Albert Bruce. A heterologous collection of cabins, and ultimately a scattering of small businesses, spread through the forest. Lumber was supplied by the Bruce sawmill run by Bert, who did the first selective cutting in the area. Most of the output was bought by Camp Curry, but he also supplied Sierra Lodge, Camp Hoyle, and the local trade. Two small mills were built on the south side of the Merced; the Quigg Mill by Jay Bruce in 1912, and Claude Roush's 1930-33 mill. Washburn and Bruce's mill had caved in from snow before 1900. Bob Bruce worked in brother Bert's mill, and Bill Bruce did carpentry so, the sons, as had their parents, contributed to the development of Wawona.

Between 1922 and '32, Camp Hoyle, run by Elsie and Bert Hoyle, stood on the site of the old Army headquarters on the ridge above Camp A.E. Wood. "Ham and Eggs, 50c" was their specialty, and sometimes Washburn himself stopped by for a meal. Furthermore, he sold them blocks of ice from Stella Lake, milk, and beef. Camp Hoyle consisted of eight tents and five cabins and catered to campers who would not have considered the hotel. After the new road was

An aerial view by an army pilot taken in December, 1925, shows the meadow, forest, hotel and, on the far clearing, Sierra Lodge. (SS Collection.)

Construction of the new (and present) Wawona Road was the dominant event from 1929 until 1932. (Hank Garber Collection.)

WAWONA LAKE
WAWONA, CALIF.

Sierra Lodge's gateway stood prominently above the end of Stella Lake in view of hotel guests who picnicked, swam and rowed boats during summer. (SS Collection.)

begun on the flat, the Hoyles built a restaurant, containing a small store, down there. A highway construction camp was set up on the same flat, and Mrs. Hoyle often fed 75 to 100 men from it daily at 50c a meal. Every morning, Frank Gallison buzzed the camp as a signal for Bert to drive to the landing field for butter, newspapers, and mail.

Camp Hoyle gave Washburn and the other directors ideas. Between the "carriage" trade who wanted hotel rooms with meals, and the campers who didn't, there were people who wanted inexpensive lodgings and food. It was determined at a 1926 Board Meeting that the Wawona Hotel should provide services to attract the in-betweeners. Accordingly, a coffee shop was built, which opened on May 27, 1926, the same day as the Sequoia Hotel, which had been converted from the L-shaped women employees' "house" built in 1920. The Sequoia operated on the European plan with rooms at moderate rates. Two days after its opening, Washburn noted "About 200 at Hotel and 38 at Sequoia." Both it and the coffee shop closed by August 24, reflecting the annual fall drop in Yosemite traffic.

On May 29, 1927, Clarence recorded, "Very heavy travel — 191 in both Hotels which is most I can remember at Wawona at one time." "Over 200 besides Sequoia" was his notation on July 14. These figures are significant because the new, paved, all-year highway 140 from Merced to Yosemite Valley had opened on July 31, 1926, and it had been expected that in response, travel on the old Wawona Road would decline drastically. Its impact on travel was hurtful, but not dramatic, for most tourists wanted to see the Mariposa Grove.

Nevertheless, Clarence was agitating for a wide, two-lane, paved highway through Wawona. As early as 1919, letters indicate that political pressure was used to induce the building of both the all-year and Wawona Roads at once. Naturally, the Camp Curry people backed the all-year route politically and financially. Survey of the Wawona route was delayed because the San Joaquin Light and Power Company held a permit to construct a dam on the South Fork. Had their plan been realized, a large part of the Wawona Basin and all the hotel property would have been flooded. After the permit (and interest) expired in 1928, surveyors of the U.S. Bureau of Public Roads went to work. They planned the new road to begin at the Park's South Entrance, extend down Big Creek to rejoin the old route at Camp Hoyle (Camp A.E. Wood), and on to the Valley. Washburn objected vigorously to having Wawona by-passed by a mile and a half. After a consultation with the directors, he "offered to donate a 100-foot right-of-way through the Wawona Hotel property if the road was located so it would pass near the hotel." It can be imagined that the offer was supported by friends with political clout, for the Bureau changed the route even though it meant building on a steeper grade.

Washburn's 1930 diary recorded progress. On July 1 he went to Yosemite and signed a letter for the right-of-way through the property, then on August 10 noted that he would sign the road deeds the next day. On October 17, he wrote, "Men started clearing right of way in front of Hotel." A large portion of the old apple orchard and the produce garden were sacrificed, but the hotel grounds did not suffer otherwise. In fact, the roadway curved around the bottom of the hill so drivers could look up to see the attractive resort. A new concrete bridge replaced the aged, often-repaired covered bridge across the South Fork.

Local highway construction, the controls it entailed, and the rains that turned it into a tire-trapping quagmire was the major event of 1930 and '31. That was reflected in declining business at the hotel, and in discouraged notations in Clarence's diary. Nationally, the stock market crash had triggered the Great Depression that dominated all lives. Washburn's diary mirrored that, too. On July 30, 1931, he recorded that he had closed both the Sequoia Hotel and the Coffee Shop because travel was "awful." Many rooms remained empty, and services such as the beauty shop and Indian Curio Shop produced little revenue. Bank notes, taken to finance the extensive improvements, had to be met; salaries, bills, and stock dividends paid. Bankruptcy was a threat. Higgins urged that the land around the meadow be subdivided, but the other directors resisted such spoilation. The alternative was to sell the Wawona Hotel and its property.

Less than a year after the Yosemite Park and Curry Co. had been formed in February, 1925, by merger of two rival concessionaires in Yosemite Valley, the new company offered to buy both the Wawona Hotel Company and the Yosemite Stage & Turnpike Co. In response, directors asked for $750,000, a prohibitive sum to the Curry interests. Finally, on March 23, 1926, the stage company was purchased for $250,000 and, according to Don Tresidder, president of the Yosemite Park and Curry Co. (YP & C Co. hereafter), "Wawona would be protected against unfair discrimination of the transportation company by a five-year contract guaranteeing Wawona all the lunch and overnight business which it had previously enjoyed. It was believed by all parties interested that the experience would form the basis of a final settlement of the Wawona question."

One tremendously interested party was the National Park Service. Park officials wanted the entire 10,000 acre Wawona Basin included in Yosemite National Park so as to stop logging, protect wildlife and watershed, control bootlegging, allow better accessibility to the lake-dotted back country, insure adequate fire protection to the Mariposa Grove, and halt further subdivision. Congress approved a bill allowing Wawona to be purchased and included in the Park by Presidential proclamation. As the Depression deepened, Washburn reluctantly offered to sell the hotel and surrounding land for $350,000. By then it was mortgaged for $100,000, and had a deficit of $160,000. Offers, counter-proposals, negotiations in Yosemite, San Francisco, and Washington, misunderstandings, intricate politics, and meeting after meeting ensued.

Politics and pressure were definite factors. Ex-World War I flyer Tresidder had a covetous eye on the Wawona airstrip, and convinced YP & C Co. directors

As general manager of the Wawona Hotel Company, Clarence Washburn had charge of everything from guests to politics. (WWH Collection.)

After Sierra Lodge closed, Sara Scroggs, who had trained under Dr. Maria Montessori and ran a Montessori school in San Francisco, bought the property and used the buildings for a children summer camp. She was a pioneer in teaching children with learning difficulties, but was forced to close the camp because of the Great Depression. (Robert G. Reese Collection.)

From parades to rodeo and fireworks, July 4 was a gala day at Wawona. Tom Gordon and Clarence Washburn are the men on the driver's seat. (SS Collection.)

that it could be developed into an asset for the Company. In contrast, Yosemite Superintendent Charles Goff Thomson, a World War I combat veteran who expected to be addressed as "Colonel," had a passion for golf. Hil Oehlmann, a close observer of the purchase problems, felt that Thomson's love of golf "was at least a contributory factor" in the Park Service push behind the acquisition. "The Colonel was a forceful and convincing individual, and strong Park superintendents carried much weight in Washington . . ."

Ultimately, on August 20, 1932, the U.S. Government agreed to pay the Wawona Hotel Company one-half the total purchase price of $150,000 in return for a deed to all its real property, i.e. the 2,665 acres, at the same time as the YP & C Co. agreed to pay the Wawona Hotel Company $85,000 for the buildings, furnishings, improvements, and operating rights. In return, the YP & C. Co. would have possessory rights of the Wawona Hotel, and a new 20-year contract with the Government as chief concessionaire in Yosemite. Six days later, President Hoover's proclamation, adding 8,785 acres of the Wawona Basin to Yosemite, was publicized. Part of that acreage had been donated by the U.S. Forest Service. Camp Hoyle was acquired for $8,000 at the same time as the Wawona Hotel sale. Only Section 35, originally the Bruce property, remained privately-owned land; and private enterprises on it catered to the public, thus reducing the impact on Yosemite Valley.

Tresidder realized that the name Washburn was synonymous with the Wawona Hotel and its long tradition of hospitality so he asked Clarence to continue as manager at $300 per month, room and board. On November 8, the day the YP & C Co. took control, Tresidder wrote Washburn:

Effective today, you are appointed Manager of all the operations in the Wawona area. I shall expect you to operate these properties for the ensuing year precisely along the lines followed by you in the past. Colonel Thomson has assured me that the Government will institute no regime in the Wawona area which will in any way alter or affect the fundamental character and atmosphere of the Wawona Hotel.

The raising of fresh vegetables, grazing of cattle, horses, etc., will continue as in the past. Rates and services for 1933 will remain the same, except as you yourself may see fit to modify them.

Our Company has a keen appreciation of the goodwill built up by the Washburns through all the years they have occupied the Wawona basin. We have no intention of endangering this goodwill by failure to continue the policies that will retain its present delightful atmosphere.

Three generations of Washburns, Estella, Clarence and Wawona, celebrated the hotel's 60th anniversary of Washburn ownership in 1934, two months before they left Wawona. (WWH Collection.)

Throughout the complicated negotiations, Superintendent Thomson had been cooperative in every way. Once the sale was complete, however, he used his position arbitrarily, quickly breaking his promise to leave the fundamental atmosphere of the hotel unchanged. Without consulting Tresidder or Washburn, he had Park Service horses quartered in the hotel's barn, put rangers in cottages formerly used by Washburn's in-laws, ordered all signs advertising the hotel removed, and granted a prime site, often used by guests, as grounds for a Civilian Conservation Corps site.

The Company's insistence, and the Park Service's pre-purchase assent, was that the Wawona operation would continue as a hotel and ranch combination. "There were cattle and milk cows, pigs and chickens, a slaughter house, vegetable gardens, and," Oehlmann added, "even homemade sausages." Thomson moved immediately "to abate those nuisances as unsuitable for a national park," and in a very short time the character of Wawona became generally similar to any other developed area in Yosemite.

As if Thomson' edicts weren't enough, the YP & C Co., burdened by the increasing Depression, cut its employees at the hotel to a minimum. Washburn at times was manager, front desk clerk, and even tended the ditch at low water times so as to maintain electricity for the hotel. Guests complained about the lack of

services, while the Curry Company screamed at the overhead, heating, and maintenance bills. Women cooks replaced the Chinese command of the kitchen. Road construction traffic controls, and a rainy spring during 1933 further harassed Washburn, who suffered, not surprisingly, from ulcers.

A YP & C Co. publicist thought it would be appropriate to celebrate the hotel's 60th Anniversary on June 16, 1934, although Henry Washburn had not acquired the property until December 26, 1874. Still, the good-for-business celebration was held, and three generations of Washburns officiated — "Mrs. John," Clarence, and his daughter, Wawona. Wawona, angry and frustrated, threatened not to participate, but her father put the situation in perspective with the quiet admonition, "This is for 60 years of Wawona, not the Washburn family, so pay your respects." She did.

By mid-summer, Washburn himself was exhausted, ill, and weary of the new, impersonal regime, the changes, the climate of competition between guest units, governmental restrictions, and red tape. Knowing the hotel was to close early in the season, he gave notice. August 28, 1934, was his last day at the place he had known, loved, and served all his 48 years. His diary entry of August 28 reflected his loyalty and dedication.

". . . Did everything possible to help them out."*

---

*Four months after he left Wawona, Washburn purchased the lease on the Hotel Potter in Indio, a thriving tourist town near Palm Springs. He took an active part in community and civic affairs both in the city and county. For 12 years he was Mayor of Indio, and in 1958 given the title of "Mr. Indio" at a testimonial dinner. After his death at age 86, September 1, 1972, the Washburn Community Center was dedicated to him. Additionally, as in Mariposa County, he was involved in the planning and development of roads in Coachella Valley. His interest in, and devotion to Wawona, remained keen, and he always enjoyed visiting the area and his old friends.

Chapter XII

Modern Times

•

Although its heaviest patronage was from transient guests, the Wawona Hotel had been a family resort, family owned and operated. After the 1934 exit of Clarence Washburn, it was run entirely by the YP & C Co., a corporation. It, too, had been founded by a family, Jennie and David Curry; and she, her daughter, Mary, and son-in-law, Don Tresidder, were still dominant, but their allegiance was to Camp Curry, Yosemite Lodge, and The Ahwahnee Hotel. Until the new Wawona Road was completed and paved, Wawona seemed remote to the Currys and other Valley residents. To them it was a way station, en route to the promised land, not a place to stay and surrender to pastoral beauty.

So it was that once acquired, the Wawona Hotel became a step-child, sometimes ignored, even unwanted; maintained but not improved. Timing of the purchase was poor because the new road had so reduced the distance and discomfort of the Yosemite trip that tourists no longer needed to stop at Wawona. Timing, in fact, couldn't have been worse because of the Depression. Net profit to the YP & C Co. of all units was only $1,495 in 1932. Little profit was derived from Wawona; in 1934 it grossed only $1,122 more than expenses.

At that time, unlike now, the complex was not considered of particular architectural merit. "The style might be called California Colonial," stated Jeannette Dyer Spencer, longtime interior designer for the Curry Company. "Its interior design was inconsistent. Random seems a good word for it." Random was an apt description of the plumbing too, and travelers of the 1930's expected better facilities than provided at Wawona. An exhaustive inventory, taken by the YP & C Co. just prior to their takeover, showed that there were 173 guest bedrooms existing in the seven buildings, but only 35 bathrooms plus a few "toilet closets." Two toilet closets off the porch, 25 washbowl-and-pitcher sets, and 24 slop jars constituted the entire sanitation "system" for the 28-room Long White. It was promptly closed as a rental unit. Even the 1917-built Annex, with 39 bedrooms, had only 20 bathrooms, and they were connecting, not private ones.

Curry personnel, sent up from the Valley, felt that the equipment, such as wood stoves in the kitchen, was antiquated, and the lighting inadequate. An eight-inch pipeline had been installed beneath the Washburn Ditch, but water still flowed through it and, when obstructed, ceased as did the power it generated.

Another minor problem to new employees was the possessive attitudes of hotel habitues who demanded favorite rooms, and tables in the dining room. Their plaint, "Things weren't run like this when the Washburns were here," was unappreciated. To their credit, the ubiquitous Gordons transferred work and loyalty to the new company because they loved the hotel. Eddie continued to be in charge of the stables, and May managed the store and post office. Son Albert was the

No baths existed in 28-room Long White, which was built in 1876, but the Yosemite Park & Curry Company closed off the attic in 1947 and made eight rooms with baths out of the 16 old ones downstairs. In 1953, the building was named Clark Cottage for pioneer innkeeper Galen Clark. (Ansel Adams photograph; YP & C Co.)

hotel engineer, daughter Gladys a maid and hostess, and Richard, the youngest, worked as a guide.

Louisiana Foster's competence and charm made her an outstanding manager after Clarence, under whom she had worked as assistant. Lou commanded loyalty, and eventually gained it from the old-time guests. She was the first of many managers who grew to love Wawona for its beguiling attributes, varied recreational pursuits, and distance from headquarters.

True, President Tresidder literally flew in and out, as he kept his private plane, which he used for business trips, at the airfield. Tresidder recorded, ". . . the Wawona purchase was based to a large extent on the assurance that a first class airport could be developed."

Don Tresidder and his sister, Oliene T. Mintzer. She managed the Wawona Hotel, exclusive of the war years, from 1940 until 1951. (YP & C Co. Collection.)

To this end, the Company had improved the golf course and "rehabilitated" the most important structures, i.e., reroofed and painted several buildings, more or less in return for airport improvement. CCC boys did grade the runway and put in drainage ditches, which were eroded by the winter run-off, but the air strip was still dangerous, and only skillful pilots used it on a limited basis.

Governmental approval, without funding, was given for a 5,000-by 500-foot runway, but the project tangled with red tape and foot dragging. Tresidder fought for the airfield until 1941 when it was finally ruled unsuitable for even emergency landings. After that, Wawona's pioneer field reverted to pasture.

What flying was to Tresidder, golfing was to Thomson. Until his death in 1937, the superintendent was wholeheartedly supportive, and used pressure for improvements to the golf course. For a while, he wanted the government to do the work and "operate the course in the same manner that municipalities do." Such a practice, of course, was foreign to Park Service goals, and he dropped the idea.

When the Company took over the Hotel, it gained possessory interest in 50 buildings and their contents. Every item, from mahogany beds to kegs of nails, had to be inventoried. Now those listings evoke pioneer days. A leather crimper and cider press were found in the stable storehouse. Stages, a buggy, a spring wagon, and 40,800 split shakes were in the wagon shed; five ice-cutting saws, and a horsepowered turntable in the ice house. The Chinese bunkhouse contained 30 folding cots, 21 blankets, 13 tables, and seven mirrors. Four pages enumerated the contents of a storage shed, which included "1 box sick room articles, 1 large piece big tree bark, 1 brass bedsteasd, and deer antlers." It took 21 pages to list items found in the general store. An adjacent smokehouse was furnished with a wood stove, a lard kettle, and combination smoke bin and corn beef press.

A few of the buildings were already obsolete, and the reduction in ranch operations made others so. Winter snow caved in the roof of the blacksmith shop; it was not replaced, as shoeing horses could be done at the stables. Also in 1933, the old boiler hosue, tent platforms, and a hide drying room were razed. In 1934, the schoolhouse was censured by the Park Service because it had broken windows, a stove that constituted a fire hazard, no water supply, and two unsanitary privies. Thomson thought the teacherage was equally deplorable. Seemingly, golfing had priority over schooling, for no money was forthcoming until 1937, when a new school was erected on the north side of the river just inside Section 35. It was, and is, used for meetings, Catholic mass, multi-purpose events, and a grammar school.

A shortsighted Park Service official decided that all the account books, guest registers, and Wawona School records on shelves in the basement of the main building were a fire hazard and ordered them destroyed. Sadly, Al Gordon trucked load after load of the priceless records to the Government dump where they were burned. Gordon, and other nostalgic employees, salvaged a few of the volumes, most of which now reside in Park Service archives.

Between 1933 and 1940, a labor force was available to the Park Service. Approximately 200 young, ablebodied though inexperienced men were in the CCC camps at Wawona, and they did manual labor in exchange for board, room, and training. Their work, and that of other groups throughout the Park, was of incalculable and lasting value to Yosemite. At and around Wawona, for example, they were responsible for razing buildings, erosion control, trail building, road work, fire fighting, and clearing logging debris from cut-over areas. The main camp, with low, one-story barracks in rows, recreational facilities, and storage buildings was built near the site of the former rodeo grounds and baseball diamond. The camp was always orderly and neat, but probably never more so than on the April, 1940, day when it was visited by America's first lady — Eleanor Roosevelt. Her uncle, Theodore, had lunched at the Wawona Hotel 37 years earlier, but she ate in the CCC camp mess hall and talked to the men.

Longest in tenure and most devoted of all the many YP & C Co. managers of the Wawona Hotel was Oliene Tresidder Mintzer, the president's sister. She ran it (exclusive of three years during World War II) from 1940 through 1950. As a young woman she had worked as an entertainer at Camp Curry and absorbed the Curry edict of "guests should be treated as if they were in your own home." Although her brother appointed her to the Wawona post, he was not supportive when she wanted money for improvements, as The Ahwahnee and Camp Curry always had priority. After closing one year, she and Eddie Gordon painted all the furniture of one room of the Long Brown (iron beds, dressers, and chairs) ivory white to show how pleasant the rooms could look. The next year a sum was allowed by the Company so all the rooms would be coordinated.

There was no hotel gardener, so she bought, and with Gordon's help, planted and watered — often late at night — columbine and other native blooms. If mint juleps needed fixing, blankets shaking, or prickly hop vines tying, Oliene would pitch in to help. "You work too hard — a good manager gives orders," Don complained, "You are a working manager." She had to be for she was manager, hostess, and entertainment director with no assistant. Guests loved her and employees, although suspicious of her power base, respected her. In 1940-41, hard-working Amos Neal was her chief clerk, and later Jean Bennett, Jr., filled that important position. Oldtimer Margaret Earls was the "wonderful, cooperative housekeeper," and a couple of good chefs plus maids, porters, and bellmen

The Wawona School was one of the 50 buildings in the hotel complex. It stood between the road and the river upstream from the covered bridge until a new one was built on the north side of the river in 1937. (YP & C Collection.)

completed her staff.

In emergencies Oliene reminisced, "I ran for Eddie Gordon. He knew everything about Wawona, and never let me down. Never." When lights blinked at night, signalling an obstruction in the ditch, "Many's the night I ran for Eddie, and then up the Brook Walk to pull pine cones out of the screen." When a guest died, "I ran for Eddie. The smile on his face when I'd arrive for the summer was a delight to me. He was a darling and so was May."

Once each summer, Oliene organized a moonlight ride to the Mariposa Grove with a stop for a barbeque, a campfire, and group singing. Some of the guests slept out afterwards, but she rode back to the hotel in the moonlight so she could supervise the next morning's activities. Sometimes Don joined the expeditions, and once commented, "I don't know how you do it, Sis." "That," Oliene said, "was the nearest he ever came to complimenting me."

After the war, guests were demanding private baths, and she pushed the idea of remodeling the bath-less Long White, which was used only for employee housing. She wanted Ted Spencer to be the architect, and his wife, Jeannette, the interior designer, as they were experts. Headquarters sat on the checkbooks, but finally, "I got them." When the Spencers and workmen were through, the attic (and its bedrooms) was closed off, and instead of 16 small rooms downstairs, there were eight medium-sized ones, each with a private bath. Each room had its own distinctive color scheme and hand-loomed rugs. The oldest building on the complex had the newest look; guests loved it, and resulting revenue soon repaid costs.

Several years later, the Long Brown was similarly remodeled; its 21 rooms altered so that there were eight

May Gordon ran the Wawona general store for years. Next to it was the Dance Hall. (YP & C. Collection.)

Stables boss, packer, stagedriver, winter caretaker, Eddie Gordon was indispensable to the Washburns and the Curry Company. (Gordon Family Collection.)

Random was one description of the Wawona Hotel's architecture, but charming summed up its setting. The new highway crosses the old Chowchilla Mountain which bends into the forest. (YP & C Co. Collection.)

upstairs and eight down, all with private baths. The "bowl and pitcher" rooms upstairs in the Main Hotel remained unchanged, but eventually, as today, used only for employees. Oliene, the chef, and the housekeeper had rooms on the view-less back until, in 1948, she persuaded headquarters that the rarely rented, three-room Little White would make logical housing for the manager. Within a short time of her move, it became known as the Manager's Cottage.

For years the University of California Alumni Houseparty took up opening week. Another annual group were 35 Bay Area people who rented the second floor of the ever-popular Annex. When groups like that descended en masse for dinner all wanting a certain table, "it took a lot of handling by the dining room crew," Oliene remembers. After 1948, the hotel was illuminated by commercial power, which meant, Oliene said, "No more cooking with wood in the summer heat, and no more lights dimming and going out at important times. No more ice cutting in early spring."

"Among my memories of happy tiems," she continued, "were evening barbeques on the back lawn, buffet lunches around the pool, guest picnics at Nelder Grove, overnight pack trips, excursions to see wildflowers, and sunsets seen from the lovely cool of the front porch." Even employees contributed to guest entertainment. At least once a week, they set up their hi-fis and played operatic and symphonic music. Their records also provided accompaniment for folk and square dances. Outdoor slide lectures by rangernaturalists were another diversion and, of course, there were the Washburn-era rocking chairs for those guests who wanted no entertainment beyond view and peace.

In contrast to the 1940's, four managers officiated in the 1950's, Howard "Duke" Doucette, Bob Maynard, John Foster Curry, grandson of Camp Curry's founders, and Nic Fiore, now Director of Winter Sports and the only one of the four still working for the Curry Co. In retrospect, Curry commented that running the Wawona Hotel was his favorite job because of its historical significance, the "unusually fine clientele," and being independent of the rest of the Company.

During Doucette's five summers, actor William Bendix was a guest as were California's Attorney General (later Governor), Edmund G. Brown, and Controller Alan Cranston, now a U.S. Senator. Brown became an enthusiastic repeat guest, and was among those that did not complain at the lack of telephones and television. Today, he writes, "The Wawona Hotel is a wonderful place. I can't think of any other site in the entire world where the setting is more magnificent . . . I have brought my family there since they were little children, and I have enjoyed it more and more as times goes by."

In 1952, Mary Curry Tresidder, Hil Oehlmann, and George Goldsworthy decided that Long White, Long Brown, and Small Brown were unimaginative names for historic buildings so they renamed them Clark Cottage, Washburn Cottage, and Moore Cottage to commemorate pioneers.

Two years later a new grocery store, grill, and coffee shop were built on the flat below the hotel; later a gas station was added. Beginning in the winter of 1956, the Annex and the Washburn Cottage (formerly the Long Brown) were kept open on weekends, mostly for skiers. Meals were available at the coffee shop.

Documentation for such business affairs exists in the YP & C Co. archives, but no personal anecdotal material has been found, and probably was not made, for the contemporary, non-pioneering years since World War II. Neither managers nor guests kept journals. Occasional mentions in the *Yosemite Sentinel*, houseorgan for the YP & C Co., news releases, and memories of people involved with Wawona have been prime sources.

The most dramatic event of the 1950's was the flood of December, 1955, best remembered for the damage to Marysville and Yuba City. Yosemite Valley, Wawona's covered bridge, and Stella Lake also suffered major injury. Even though the bridge had not been used for vehicle traffic since 1931, it was still an important passageway for pedestrians and equestrians, as a link between the hotel and the stables. As the only covered bridge in a national park, it deserved preservation, and money was allocated by the National Park Service. Emergency cribbing maintained it during 1956, and that winter the entire structure was placed on rollers and winched onto the north bank where careful reconstruction took place before it was eased back to bridge the river.

From 1964 on, it was to serve not only as a link to the past, but focal point of a pioneer village where abandoned historic buildings, from various places in Yosemite, were moved, restored, and used as living history exhibits. Ultimately Camp A.E. Wood's Army headquarters, a Wells Fargo building, a schoolhouse, an old stone jail, a pioneer home, an artist's studio, old barns, a blacksmith shop, and a large collection of vintage vehicles were set in place on both sides of the river. Once again horse-drawn stages thunder through the bridge with passengers jammed happily on the seats, enjoying the atmosphere of yesterday. In the History Center, they can attend school, listen to a uniformed U.S. Cavalryman, watch a blacksmith work, or participate in other vital and valid living history programs.

During the flood, a gaping hole developed in the bank below Stella Lake and was never repaired. Today, the old lake site is a derelict pit indicating none of the beauty or usage it supplied for so many years. The Brook Walk along the verdant banks of the Washburn Ditch fared little better. It too was damaged when high waters surged through it. The YP & C Co. urged its re-establishment on the basis of history and guest

Golfing on the first course in the Sierra Nevada was a delight to hotel guests and the Yosemite Superintendent. (WWH Collection.)

enjoyment, but the Park Service felt its use would be a possible hazard, difficult, and expensive to maintain. Eddie Gordon and Frank Marks, a property owner, did enough work so water ran through it, at least in 1962, but the Park Service stopped that, as well as efforts to activate it in 1976 and '77.

From 1961 through 1966, continuity, in the persons of Agnes and Cy Wright, reigned at the Wawona Hotel. After a number of years of work at Camp Curry, the couple bought the El Capitan Hotel in Merced and ran it for 12 years. In May of 1961, they returned to the mountains, Cy as manager, and Agnes as chief clerk at Wawona. No sooner had the doors opened on May 26 than 100 architects registered, followed, in quick succession, by a group of hotel executives, the Horseless Carriage Club, and the Cal Alumni. In times of crisis, Cy could fill in at any task, even to flipping pancakes, and soon won the approval of staff, guests, and YP & C Co. general manager Hil Oehlmann. Wright, said Oehlmann "was a perfectionist, and in his quiet way, brought every facet of quality and service to the optimum standard which the old, but refurbished resort could achieve. The golf course was greatly improved, and the cuisine was improved to the point where it received recognition as an outstanding dining room." Wright did what he could to enhance and restore the historical character of the hotel, but

welcomed a complete renovation of the kitchen from sagging floor to smoke-grimed ceiling. About $20,000 of the $85,000 expense was for modern equipment.

Agnes "was a gracious, quiet, efficient lady . . . an ideal helpmate to Cy." It was she who saw that small Christmas trees were decorated and placed in children's rooms. When the power went off one Christmas, it was she who suggested serving ingenious toast-on-forks meals around the cobblestone fireplace.

The Wrights had able, loyal backup from longtime Curry Company employees, particularly Rosella Armstrong, as a clerk under Agnes, and Homer Armstrong, the meticulous superintendent of the golf course. Even today the Armstrongs serve visitors at the Mariposa Grove where she is chief dispatcher of the public trams. Another couple of value to Wawona were the Martins; Addie, the hotel's housekeeper, who attended to such diverse needs as supplying cribs and searching for false teeth. Her husband, George, better known as Buck, was the maintenance man who, with tools and prayer, kept the worn facilities operating.

Charlie Eagle, resident golf pro for years, was a favorite with guests and Yosemite residents who had long since organized a golf club and tournaments. Often convention managers picked Wawona as a site because of the golf course. That caused problems with hardcore conservationists. Was the course compatible with a National Park? Its placement, age, and attractiveness won out. Next there was a flap over the introduction of golf carts. Were they compatible? That question was academic after 1957 when some golfers brought their own electric carts. In fact the outcry from investment banker Jean Witter and others was for adequate power to recharge carts. It was 1967 before YP & C Co. was allowed to buy, maintain, and rent vehicles to serve golfers.

In 1978, the Park Service abruptly removed a long section of the old rail fence to reuse in Yosemite Valley. Eleven days later, because of public and concessionaire outcry, the fencing was returned to its proper, historical home.

Wawona Washburn Hartwig wrote "Wawona has long been recognized . . . as a uniquely beautiful spot, in large part due to the picturesque rail-fenced meadow and green golf course . . . It has been in continuous use since the spring of 1918. Its beauty, and the delight of watching deer graze upon it, has added to the enjoyment of thousands of people going to and from Yosemite Valley."

In the late 1960's and early 1970's, city-type ills beset Yosemite Valley, but Wawona remained remote and peaceful. Deer and people were compatible; stage and horseback rides available; golfing, fishing, swimming, and hiking as popular as ever. After the Wrights retired as managers, Duke Doucette returned briefly, followed by Earl Pomeroy, Bill Wismer, Dillon Gillis, John Sibel, Ivan Neiman, Glen Power, Gillis again, and since 1976, Bob LaCroix. These able but transitory managers were assisted by more permanent staff, notably the Armstrongs, Martins, Coletha and Paul Jones, and Chuck Whitewolf. Their loyalty and stewardship helped keep the hotel functioning smoothly.

After Thomas Hill's death in 1908, his studio was used at different times, for storage, soda fountain, and a recreation hall for employees. It had architectural dignity, but no lasting identity. In 1962, Hill's youngest daughter, Flora Hill McCullough, 83, advised the Park Service on her father's life and work as well as the Studio's original design and furnishings. Legal and budgeting wheels ground very slowly but, finally in 1967, work to restore the historical character of the building was done by Park Service. Since then the Studio has been furnished appropriately, and opened summers as a living history unit.

On Thanksgiving Day, 1977, a disgruntled ex-employee, who had already burned two structures in Yosemite Valley, set fire to the Sequoia building, which burned rapidly. Fortunately, the hotel had closed for the winter and firemen kept the flames from spreading to the other buildings. Unfortunately, 41 rooms of furniture plus some belongings of employees were lost, as was the building itself.

After consultations with Park Service personnel, Ed Hardy, chief operating officer of the YP & C Co., ar-

An arsonist destroyed the Sequoia Hotel building on Thanksgiving Day, 1977. (YP & C Co. Collection.)

ranged for many employees to live in a former motel across the river, others, as usual, upstairs in the main building, and still others in the Moore Cottage, which had been closed for several years. A new roof, new stairway railings, plumbing fixtures, some foundation work, and a coat of white paint returned the old structure to use in May, 1978.

Since 1932, Section 35, an inholding, has been a mixed blessing to the Park Service. Small subdivisions have caused a proliferation of vacation and permanent homes, as well as small businesses. These have led to sanitation and control problems. However, motels and restaurants catering to the public have taken some of the burden off the facilities in Yosemite Valley. During 1977 and part of 1978, the Park Service instituted a program of harassment and threatened condemnation that led to determined opposition and even organization of private property owners.

As this book is being written, plans are underway to celebrate the 100th anniversary of the main hotel building on May 13, 1979, with various and appropriate ceremonies. Galen Clark and Henry Washburn, founders of the Wawona Hotel will be recalled, and Wawona Washburn Hartwig, third-generation descendant of the pioneering brothers, and Hester Bruce Stephan and Albert Gordon, also members of historic Wawona families, will be honored guests — at home once more in an ageless, yet aged, place of beauty, charm, and peace.

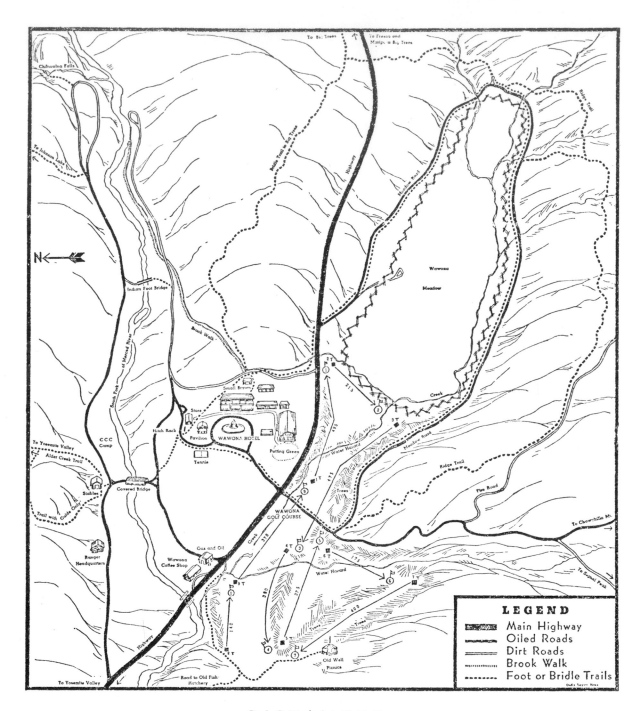

DISTANCES

	miles		miles
Meadow Loop Road	3.5	Ridge Trail—(Loop around meadow, returning to Hotel.	5.4
Brook Walk—(each way)	2.0		
		To Johnson Lake	11.1
Ridge Trail—(Wawona Hotel to Mariposa Grove of Big Trees)	5.9	To Yosemite Valley—(via Alder Creek Trail)	19.5

A 1933 map of the Wawona area indicates some of its attractions.

Index

*Denotes Illustration

Index Continued